THE GLOBAL ECONOMIC CRISIS AND MIGRATION

WHERE DO WE GO FROM HERE?

Bimal Ghosh

2010

IOM International Organization for Migration

The Hague Process on Refugees and Migration

Table of contents

List of figures and tables

Acronyms and abbreviations

ADB	Asian Development Bank
EBRD	European Bank for Reconstruction and Development
ECB	European Central Bank
FAO	Food and Agriculture Organization of the United Nations
FDI	Foreign direct investment
GDP	Gross domestic product
ILO	International Labour Organization
IMF	International Monetary Fund
IOM	International Organization for Migration
MDG	Millennium Development Goals
NGO	Non-governmental organization
OECD	Organisation for Economic Co-operation and Development
UNDP	United Nations Development Programme
WTO	World Trade Organization

Foreword

The corrosive effects of the Great Recession – the worst since the 1930s – on labour markets and workforces are now widely known. These, in turn, are driving changes in migration policies and patterns – changes that can significantly influence social peace, inter-state relations, and the pace of global economic recovery. Yet these migration issues have thus far received little attention, with recession-related policy debates and public discussions mostly focused on financial rules and reform. Into this void comes Bimal Ghosh's new book, jointly sponsored by the International Organization for Migration (IOM) and The Hague Process on Refugees and Migration, which bridges the policy gap and offers a fresh outlook on the future of migration.

In exploring the recession's impact on migration policies and patterns, Professor Ghosh examines the decline in economic growth – including international trade, capital flows, development aid, and remittances – and analyses its links to joblessness and incomes, poverty and inequality, and changes in the labour force. The discussion draws on experiences of past recessions showing that job-market recovery takes longer than economic recovery. He then examines how these trends – and government reactions to them in both rich and poor countries – have been influencing migration overall.

What might be the recession's impact on migration patterns in origin and destination countries? The portents are many. For instance, destination countries might restrain new immigration in line with falling labour demand. When such measures are driven by panic or populist pressures and impose undue and indiscriminate restrictions on immigration, countries could pay a heavy price in future growth. Of course, such constraints could hurt origin countries as well.

Although irregular migration has fallen during the recession, Professor Ghosh argues that this trend could rapidly reverse if poorer countries are slow to recover. In the absence of opportunities for legal entry, those seeking to emigrate are most likely to opt for irregular channels, encouraging smugglers and traffickers.

Other worrisome trends also are cause for concern: In times of economic difficulty, tolerance of foreigners tends to decline. As competition for jobs and resources increases, the black economy expands and the social underclass of irregular migrants grows; the danger of discrimination rises, too. There are already signs of this in many countries. Worse still, the author adds, if this leads to widespread resentment of foreigners and gives rise to xenophobia, it could sow the seeds of social conflict and tension in inter-state relations.

None of these potential dangers is inevitable, says Professor Ghosh, and they can be minimized through timely preventive measures. He proposes insightful, well-articulated measures including: the adoption of flexible immigration policies congruent with current and anticipated labour needs; the avoidance of populist, inward-looking policies, including trade protectionism; and proactive labour-market measures. Special emphasis is laid on direct job creation. He also urges origin countries to anticipate and prepare for an increase in return migration, by establishing programmes for those who wish to resettle at home, as well as for those who seek to be redeployed when recovery begins.

For poor countries heavily dependent on remittances, meanwhile, Professor Ghosh makes a powerful plea for earmarking quickly deliverable international funds to help them tide over current imbalances. He also stresses the more effective use of remittances, alongside intensive efforts to diversify sources of external financial inflows.

Bimal Ghosh ends his book with thoughts on how nations can turn the present crisis into a great opportunity for laying the basis for the sound management of human mobility in the future. He urges countries to press ahead and develop an agreed framework of multilateral cooperation to improve the governance of human movement – just as they have been striving to do, in the wake of the recession, to better manage global financial flows.

Academics, policymakers and professionals, as well as civil society actors, will find this thoughtful, forward-looking, and lucidly written study valuable as a reference to better understand the impact of current and future economic crises on migration and the possible ways of responding to it.

As fellow members of The Club of The Hague on Refugees and Migration, we encourage their reflection on it.

Peter Sutherland
United Nations Special
Representative on Migration
and Development

William Swing
Director General, IOM

Preface

In 2009, at the height of the global economic crisis, several international organizations, including the IOM and THP, grew increasingly concerned about the impact of the crisis on international migration. It was already recognized that the worst economic meltdown since the Great Depression was bound to have serious repercussions on world migration. Less clear was how exactly this would affect the origin and destination countries in both short and near term and what should be the specific policy responses to meet the challenge. The two organizations asked me to carry out a comprehensive analysis of the issues involved and explore the ways to address them. The present book complies with their request.

Much of the book was written while the recession was still unfolding and in its immediate aftermath. As the work progressed, I made presentations on the subject at an event held in conjunction with the United Nations General Assembly's Special Session on the economic crisis and at the World Bank in Washington, D.C., the European Union in Brussels and the IOM in Geneva, as well as at various university centres. I greatly benefited from these discussions, and would like to thank all those who so kindly organized these meetings.

The recession has ended, but not the job crisis; and the tensions in international migration continue unabated. Given this still evolving situation, and in an attempt to bring the reader up to date, I have included in the book more recent information than was available at the time of my initial writing. Some of this additional information is also provided in the three Annexes to the book, the last quarter of 2010 being used as the cut-off date.

Chapter 1 of the book starts with a detailed discussion of the world economic background that shaped the recent recession and explains the dynamics and ramifications of the crisis. The discussion seeks to discern its effects on jobs, wages and workforces, including trends in poverty and inequality worldwide. This is followed in chapter 2 by an analysis of its impact on the pattern and policies of international migration. Chapter 3 then takes up the question of how these changes are likely to affect migrant-sending and migrant-receiving countries and the world economy. This leads to chapter 4, which puts forward a set of specific policy and operational measures to meet the potential perils and pitfalls embedded in the recession-driven changes in migration.

The book concludes with a look at the future of world migration. It foresees an increase in South-South migration over time alongside a gradual lessening of tension in South-North migration. Drawing a parallel with ongoing efforts in the global financial sector, it urges nations to cooperate more closely to address the current challenge of migration, and move towards the adoption of a multilateral agreement to better manage human mobility in future.

I am deeply thankful to William Swing, Director General of IOM, Peter Sutherland, United Nations Special Representative on Migration and Development, and Frans Bouwen, director of external relations at THP, for their keen interest in the study. Several officials in IOM's Research and Publications Unit provided valuable assistance in making the text ready for publication. I am thankful to Kerstin Lau, who diligently prepared the list of references; to Julia Schad, who used her organizational skills to bring together the various parts of the text and followed up on many issues during the book's production; to Joseph Rafanan, for designing the publication layout; and to Janice Ruth de Belen, for editing the text. My special thanks go to Valerie Hagger for overseeing the whole process and helping out at the final stages of publication, and for doing so with great efficiency and while dealing with a heavy workload.

The views expressed in the book, including the recommendations made, are my own, and the responsibility for any errors of omission or commission rests with me alone.

I. The crisis and its distinctive features: How different is it from its predecessors?

"Man cannot bathe twice in the same water in a running stream" is an old saying, attributed to Herodotus, the Greek historian, dating back to 400 B.C. No matter the source, this saying continues to hold sway. History is indeed a running stream, as it has always been. If it repeats itself, it does not do so in exactly the same way; "at best it rhymes", as Mark Twain put it. Since before the Great Depression, the world has seen several economic crises. However, no two of them have been exactly alike. The recent recession, clearly the worst in several decades, is not an exception. History can nonetheless be useful in understanding the present, and can keep us alive to differences between current events and their predecessors. How then does the present economic crisis differ from the Great Depression or from more recent recessions?

A striking feature of the 2008–2009 downturn is the unprecedented speed and spread of its contagion effect, which flows from the nature of the current phase of economic globalization. It is markedly different from the economically shallow and geographically narrow pre-First World War globalization, on the back of which the Great Depression took place and dominated the early 1930s.

During the earlier phase of globalization, the core of the global economy was still confined to a few countries, and their links extended mostly to colonial peripheries. Now, not only has the core economy itself become wider and diversified, but an increasing number of countries, both large and small, are actively engaged in the global economy. The Group of Seven most industrialized countries (G7) is being overshadowed, though yet to be completely dethroned, by the Group of Twenty (G20), which now includes many emerging economies from around the world and accounts for nearly 90 per cent of the world's gross domestic product (GDP) and 80 per cent of world trade. Emerging markets alone now represent more than a third of global output at market prices and may account for as much as half of global output within the next several decades. New groupings of countries such as the BRIC (Brazil, Russia, India and China), which holds 40 per cent of the world's currency reserves and accounts for about 40 per cent of the world's population (though the group accounts for just 15% of global GDP), are seeking to at least symbolically throw their weight around.

The spread and speed of the contagion effect of the crisis and the closely interwoven global economy

If the geographical scope of globalization has changed, so has the nature of economic integration, including the speed and intensity of cross-border transactions, making the system closely interlocked. In the earlier phase of economic integration, a number of countries established economic links mainly through the expansion of primary exports and flows of foreign direct investment (FDI) in the primary sector; this included transport (e.g. steamships and railways) needed for trade in primary goods (Ghosh, 1999). The economic landscape has now radically changed, with a complex web of production and supply links extending to the manufacturing and services sectors, helped by rapid technological progress. Profound changes in communication and information technology have virtually abolished distance in time and space, thereby increasing tradability and facilitating immediate delivery of a wide range of services, including those in the financial sector. Other developments, such as the 24-hour opening of the global money market and rapid expansion of e-commerce, have followed. Global data traffic nearly tripled in 2008 and 2009 and is set to double annually over the next five years as more people seek mobile Internet access via laptops and smart phones (*Financial Times,* 2010e).

Financial markets, in particular, have become closely integrated. The stock of foreign assets and liabilities relative to GDP has risen five times in the past 30 years in rich countries and by twofold in emerging economies. At the same time, the speed and intensity of financial transactions has dramatically increased: Just before the present economic crisis, every 24 hours, over USD 3 trillion were flowing across borders. Innovation in exotic financial products, including credit derivatives and mortgage-backed securities, helped to make the financial market incredibly agile and potentially volatile. Securitization of mortgage-backed debt led to a massive expansion of loans. While world GDP was less than USD 60 trillion, the derivatives market had reached USD 600 trillion, according to one estimate. In terms of the number of persons and intensity of movement, human mobility was also at a record high. Every minute, at least 13 persons, on average, were crossing borders worldwide, not counting many more people – tourists, temporary service providers and others – who are not normally considered as migrants.

Internal economic integration has progressed in a large number of countries alongside the interpenetration of markets across countries. A complex web of linkages has thus made the world economy so densely interwoven that the malfunctioning of any small part can affect the system, sending shock waves almost everywhere.

Given this fast-moving and densely interwoven economic landscape, it is no wonder that what started as a sub-prime mortgage downturn in the housing market of the United States so quickly moved to its credit market and its banking system. It then spread to manufacturing, and soon thereafter to nearly all of the real economy, leaving millions of people both homeless and jobless and causing a sharp fall in output, income and trade. Within a short span of time, this downturn became one of the severest global recessions in decades. In the last quarter of 2008 and the first quarter of 2009, the rate of downturn in advanced economies was similar to the GDP free fall in the early stages of the Depression (Roubini, 2009). A study by Eichengreen and O'Rourke (2010) found that global trade, industrial production and the stock market all saw steeper declines in 2008–2009, compared to 1929–1930.

The geographical spread is much wider this time. Not surprisingly, those who had imagined or hoped that the economic downturn would remain confined to advanced economies were soon proven wrong. Even some of the fastest-growing countries such as Brazil, China and India witnessed declines in growth and faced some serious economic difficulties with ominous social consequences. As Skidelsky (2009) put it, up until mid-2008, there was considerable Schadenfreude in emerging markets as the giants of the world economy toppled. However, after mid-2008, this confidence started to fade too. Despite being least integrated with the global economy, sub-Saharan Africa was unable to escape from the contagion fallout, and the region's poor were among the hardest hit.

It is not just the changed economic landscape that makes the recent economic crisis different from the Great Depression. An asymmetry in the sequence of events surrounding the two crises also makes them different.

Although the Depression began with a tightening of monetary policy in 1928, accelerating the American stock market collapse in 1929, many of the international economic linkages established across nations in 1870 and 1913 had been already weakened or severed. The situation was worsened by a litany of protectionist measures that followed. This included restrictionist immigration policies – notably measures in the early 1920s – that the United States introduced during and after the First World War. In the decade prior to 1929, the average flow of 400,000 permanent immigrants a year fell to half the average annual flow of 800,000 during the pre-War years (1900–1914) (OECD, 2009). It took some three years for the United States to get ready to take any effective remedial action. As Kennedy (1999) put it: "Down to the last weeks of 1930, Americans could plausibly assume that they were caught up in yet another of the routine business cycle downswings."

On 5 September 1929, economist Roger Babson, then a solitary and often disdained figure, reiterated his doomsday cry: "Sooner or later a crash is coming, and it may be terrific." As the stock market showed the first signs of fragility, then US President Herbert Hoover turned to Thomas W. Lamont, a senior partner at J.P. Morgan & Co, for reassurance. Only five days before the market virtually imploded on so-called Black Thursday, 24 October 1929, Lamont had sent his reply: "The future appears brilliant" (*The New York Times*, 2009h). From September 1930 to May 1933, President Hoover continued with his half-hearted, and mostly laissez-faire, policy, while the US economy headed towards a GDP decline of 27 per cent and unemployment soared to 25 per cent. In September 1929, the hugely inflated Dow Jones Index peaked at 381; in 1932, it declined to 41.2, reflecting a drop of 90 per cent (Skidelsky, 2009). By 1931, the recession had already turned into a serious depression.

When action finally came, it was mostly uncoordinated and local, not global. In his first inaugural speech, US President Franklin Roosevelt declared: "Our international trade relations, though vastly important, are in point of time and necessity secondary to the establishment of a sound national economy. I favor as a practical policy the putting of first things first" (Roosevelt, 1938). As an adviser to President Roosevelt famously put it: "The crisis is global, but action must be local." A breakdown of the international system soon followed. In the words of Kindleberger (1973):

> The world economic system was unstable unless some country stabilized it as Britain had done in the nineteenth century and up to 1913. In 1929, the British couldn't, and the United States wouldn't. When every country turned to protect its national private interest, the world public interest went down the drain, and with it the private interests of all.

By contrast, the recent recession neither started in an unduly protectionist environment, nor was it immediately accentuated by restrictive measures. If anything, market forces, especially in the financial sector, were in many ways allowed excessive freedom to run amok, sowing the seeds of backlash, breakdown of confidence and economic meltdown. True, ominous new signs of protectionism in many forms have since been looming large, but they gained further ground only after the recession had already set in. At least in policy rhetoric, though not necessarily in action, most nations remained committed to shunning protectionism. The emphasis, especially in Europe and the developing regions, has been more on regulatory reforms to curb market excesses and on improved transparency.

There are important institutional differences too (Bernanke, 1983; IMF, 2009; Kindleberger, 1973; Romer, 2009). For instance, in the absence of any deposit insurance schemes during the Great Depression, there were frantic bank runs, reflecting people's concerns about the solvency of their banks. As a result, the deposit base of these banks was eroded. In the United States, four waves of such runs led to the failure of a third of all banks, and the panic soon spread to other major economies – notably Austria and Germany. In the present crisis, this has been largely prevented by the existence of deposit insurance schemes. The erosion of liquidity and credit stemmed from defaults in the sub-prime mortgage markets and the falling net worth of intermediary institutions. Further, in the present crisis, the existing, flexible international monetary system has not been an obstacle to effective reflationary policy responses. In the 1930s, rigid adherence to the regime of gold exchange standard and related policy failures prevented governments from taking timely action for expansionary monetary adjustment (IMF, 2009).

A most important difference in the situation this time is the much shorter delay within which governments intervened to fight the recession and the relatively concerted manner in which they have done so. As *The Economist* (2009c) put it, it was "the biggest, broadest and fastest government response in history." This was not the case in 1929–1933, when there was a virtual breakdown of the international system.

Admittedly, as we will further discuss in this study, there were important differences in approach and the consequent tensions between governments, notably between the United States and most of Europe, in dealing with the crisis. The United States and the United Kingdom (in the initial stages, before the change of government) were more aggressive in using both fiscal and financial means to fight the recession and speed up recovery. By contrast, most of the rest of Europe were more concerned about fiscal stability, on fears that excessive deficit financing could lead to unmanageable inflation. Thus, the issue of an exit strategy from excessive monetary liquidity became a subject of intense debate. Nonetheless, these countries basically followed a similar path and the differences were more a matter of emphasis than of substance.

Despite some initial discordant posturing and even bickering in their summit meetings in London (April 2009) and Pittsburgh (September 2009), G20 leaders made a significant advance towards macroeconomic policy coordination in response to the crisis, as well as towards the adoption of a common strategy, including "shared policy objectives" to secure sustainable recovery. As part of the process, they agreed to set out national policy frameworks by January 2010 and conduct "cooperative mutual assessment" of country performances.

As of this writing, the results of such actions are yet to be known, but these joint decisions clearly marked a remarkable departure from what happened during the Depression of the 1930s. At the Toronto meeting in June 2010, differences among G20 leaders resurfaced as they debated a common strategy for further economic recovery. Some leaders emphasized the urgency of fiscal consolidation and more aggressive debt management, while others felt that, given the continuing fragility of the global economy, growth-oriented fiscal and monetary policies should remain in place. However, G20 leaders found a compromise in a common flexible approach that allowed governments to pursue fiscal consolidation at a pace that was consistent with growth. Cooperative assessment of national policy frameworks was maintained and policy coordination, if somewhat enfeebled, continued.

The deepest and most global recession of all since the 1930s

If several of the characteristics of the 2008–2009 recession differed from those of the Great Depression, how does it compare with more recent global recessions? Using standard statistical methods, the International Monetary Fund (IMF) has identified four major troughs in the past 50 years, namely in 1975, 1982, 1991 and 2009, when world real GDP per person declined. The economic turbulence of 1997–1998 and 2001 were not included since the world GDP per person did not decline during these periods. In 1997–1998, many emerging economies, particularly in Asia, experienced sharp economic declines, but growth in rich countries held up, and world real income per person did not fall. Conversely, in 2001, many rich countries suffered a mild economic downturn, but growth in major emerging economies such as China and India remained robust. In both cases, the impact of the downturn was mainly confined to certain geographical areas and was therefore less global.

In its analysis, the IMF looked at the most recent and previous recessions by applying a set of indicators of global activity: real GDP per person, industrial output, trade, capital flows, oil consumption and unemployment (see Table 1).[1] Although all these episodes of recession share a common pattern of contraction, they also reveal that the 2008–2009 recession was the severest of all. All indicators at the height of these recessions revealed a sharper decline in 2009, compared to the average decline during the three previous downturns. The difference was particularly striking for trade, capital flows and output per person.

Another striking feature of the situation is that the geographical spread of the downturn expanded significantly over the four global recessions.

[1] Based on estimates and forecasts of peaks of the four recessions.

The 2008–2009 recession stood out as the most global and the most synchronized, as nearly all the advanced economies and most emerging and developing countries were affected. Significantly, on 10 March 2009, in a speech in the United Republic of Tanzania, Dominique Strauss Kahn, the IMF managing director, called the downturn the "Great Recession";[2] the term is now widely used to describe the crisis.

Table 1: Comparison of recent recessions

Global recessions: Selected indicators of economic activity
(Percentage change, unless otherwise indicated)

Variable	1975	1982	1991	Projected 2009	Average (1975, 1982, 1991)
Output					
Per capital output (PPP[1]-weighted)	-0.13	-0.89	-0.18	-2.50	-0.40
Per capital output (market-weighted)	-0.33	-1.08	-1.45	-3.68	-0.95
Other macroeconomic indicators					
Industrial production	-1.60	-4.33	-0.09	-6.23	-2.01
Total trade	-1.87	-0.69	4.01	-11.75	0.48
Capital flows[2]	0.56	-0.76	-2.07	-6.18	-0.76
Oil consumption	-0.90	-2.87	0.01	-1.50	-1.25
Unemployment[3]	1.19	1.61	0.72	2.56	1.18
Components of output					
Per capita consumption	0.41	-0.18	0.62	-1.11	0.28
Per capita investment	-2.04	-4.72	-0.15	-8.74	-2.30

Source: IMF, April 2009.
Notes:
The 1991 recession lasted until 1993, using market weights; all other recessions lasted one year.
[1] PPP = purchasing power parity.
[2] Refers to change in the two-year rolling window average of the ratio of inflows plus outflows to GDP.
[3] Refers to percentage point change in the rate of unemployment.

1.1 Migration and economic and social realities

Migration has always closely interacted with prevailing social and economic realities in countries of origin and destination. Migration movements invariably entail both benefits and costs, which are often differentially shared between and within countries. Generally, however, in times of prosperity or

[2] Speech at a meeting of African political and financial leaders on 10 March 2009 in Dar es Salaam. Note that there is no strict definition of "depression" and that the spread and severity of the recent economic crisis dwarfed the commonly accepted US definition of a recession as at least two consecutive quarters of falling GDP.

economic reconstruction, destination countries welcome migrants. Migrants allow destination countries to meet rising labour demand, restrain wage-push inflation, boost consumption and put the economy on an upward swing. Labour-abundant sending countries respond positively – with some rare and largely ineffective exceptions as experienced in the past – to such demand in order to lessen their burden of unemployment and earn much-needed foreign exchange in the form of remittances. Driven by the supply-push of labour, sending countries tend to become more proactive in times of economic distress and high unemployment, but less so when times are bad in destination countries, and try to reabsorb returnees.

When erstwhile destination countries run into economic difficulty and others flourish and open up job opportunities, migration is diverted to new destination countries. In the wake of the first oil crisis of 1973, Western Europe somewhat suddenly banned all labour immigration. At the same time, however, the economies of oil-producing Gulf States were opening up, creating some 5 million new job opportunities. Migrants, especially those from Asia, often helped by their governments, quickly changed trajectory and massively moved to the Gulf States.

But what happens when economic woes afflict all potential destination and sending countries at the same time as part of a severe global economic crisis, as was the case in 2008–2009? When this happens, the situation becomes more complex, making it much more difficult to foresee changes in the configuration of migration or how these changes are likely to influence future growth and global recovery. For sure, past experiences can give us some useful leads, but they can also be false or misleading unless tested against new economic and social trends, for, as we have seen, each economic crisis has its own characteristics. If the most recent recession is markedly different from the Great Depression, it also stands far apart from previous recessions in the past 50 years, especially as concerns the spread, depth and speed of the economic downturn. A plausible assessment of the impact of the ongoing crisis on migration and its consequences on future recovery must therefore start with a closer look at the economic and social ramifications of the recession and its dynamics. This is attempted in the next section.

1.2 Ramifications and dynamics of the downturn

In October 2008, the IMF foresaw the world economy "entering a major downturn" as it faced "the most dangerous shock" to the rich-country financial system since the 1930s. IMF forecast a 3 per cent decline in global growth, measured in terms of purchasing power parity, in 2009, compared with a positive growth of 5.2 per cent in 2007. However, as 2009 wore on and the global economic malaise spread, the Fund downgraded its forecasts several times. Its forecast in April 2009 (see Table 2, column A) suggested that, instead of experiencing positive growth, the world economy would shrink by 1.3 per cent in 2009 and advanced economies would decline by 3.8 per cent. Emerging and developing economies were expected to grow by only 1.6 per cent in the same year, compared with 6 per cent in 2008.

Soon thereafter, as more information for the first quarter of 2009 became available, analysts foresaw an even grimmer situation, especially for the euro area. Although cautiously a little more optimistic than in April 2009, the IMF in July 2009 reduced its growth rate projections for 2009 by 0.1 per cent for the world and by 0.6 per cent for the euro area (see Table 2, column B). Others, however, were even more pessimistic. For example, the World Bank projected a 2 per cent decline in global output for 2009, while the Organisation for Economic Co-operation and Development (OECD) forecast a decline of 4.3 per cent for advanced economies, as against the 3.8 per cent decline foreseen by the IMF.

Even more disquietingly, annualized growth figures for the first quarter of 2009 in the United States implied a sharp decline of 6.2 per cent, compared with the IMF forecast of 2.6 per cent and the Congressional Budget Office's earlier projection of 2.2 per cent. Prior to 2009, only three times since the Great Depression had the US economy contracted by more than 6 per cent. The German economy shrank by 4 per cent in the first quarter of 2009, compared with the last three months of 2008. It was feared that if the decline continued at the same rate, the German economy would be a fifth smaller by the end of 2009. As for Japan, then the world's second-largest economy, its GDP fell 3.3 per cent quarter-on-quarter in the last three months of 2008; this decline was equivalent to an annualized fall of more than double the IMF's April 2009 forecast of 6.2 per cent (see Table 2, column A).

However, by mid-2009, the situation was changing. In October 2009, the IMF reduced its projections on the decline of world output to 1.1 per cent for 2009 and raised its forecast for 2010 to positive growth of 3.1 per cent (see Table 2, column C). Forecasts of declines in advanced economies for 2009 were also downgraded, although figures were slightly higher for the United States. Growth for 2010 was forecast to be higher for advanced economies as well as for emerging and developing economies.

Figures for the second and third quarters of 2009 generally confirmed this trend in several major economies. After having fallen for four consecutive quarters, the GDP of the United States expanded at an annualized rate of 3.5 per cent in the three months ended September 2009, although many analysts attributed this growth largely to government support and questioned its sustainability. In Europe, the region's two biggest economies, France and

Table 2: World economic projections (April 2009–January 2010)

Percentage change, year over year, unless otherwise noted

Projections as of:	A Apr-09				B Jul-09			C Oct-09			D Jan-10		
	2007	2008	Projections		2008	Projections		2008	Projections		2008	Projections	
			2009	2010		2009	2010		2009	2010		2009	2010
World output[1]	5.2	3.2	-1.3	1.9	3.1	-1.4	2.5	3.0	-1.1	3.1	3.0	-0.8	3.9
Advanced economies	2.7	0.9	-3.8	0.0	0.8	-3.8	0.6	0.6	-3.4	1.3	0.5	-3.2	2.1
USA	2.0	1.1	-2.8	0.0	1.1	-2.6	0.8	0.4	-2.7	1.5	0.4	-2.5	2.7
Euro area	2.7	0.9	-4.2	-0.4	0.8	-4.8	-0.3	0.7	-4.2	0.3	0.6	-3.9	1.0
Germany	2.5	1.3	-5.6	-1.0	1.3	-6.2	-0.6	1.2	-5.3	0.3	1.2	-4.8	1.5
France	2.1	0.7	-3.0	0.4	0.3	-3.0	0.4	0.3	-2.4	0.9	0.3	-2.3	1.4
Italy	1.6	-1.0	-4.4	-0.4	-1.0	-5.1	-0.1	-1.0	-5.1	0.2	-1.0	-4.8	1.0
Spain	3.7	1.2	-3.0	-0.7	1.2	-4.0	-0.8	0.9	-3.8	-0.7	0.9	-3.6	-0.6
Japan	2.4	-0.6	-6.2	0.5	-0.7	-6.0	1.7	-0.7	-5.4	1.7	-1.2	-5.3	1.7
UK	3.0	0.7	-4.1	-0.4	0.7	-4.2	0.2	0.7	-4.4	0.9	0.5	-4.8	1.3
Canada	2.7	0.5	-2.5	1.2	0.4	-2.3	1.6	0.4	-2.5	2.1	0.4	-2.6	2.6
Other advanced economies	4.7	1.6	-4.1	0.6	1.6	-3.9	1.0	1.6	-2.1	2.6	1.7	-1.3	3.3
Newly industrialized Asian economies	5.7	1.5	-5.6	0.8	1.5	-5.2	1.4	1.5	-2.4	3.6	1.7	-1.2	4.8
Emerging and developing economies[2]	8.3	6.1	1.6	4.0	6.0	1.5	4.7	6.0	1.7	5.1	6.1	2.1	6.0
Africa	6.2	5.2	2.0	3.9	5.2	1.8	4.1	5.2	1.7	4.0	5.2	1.9	4.3
Sub-Sahara	6.9	5.5	1.7	3.8	5.5	1.5	4.1	5.5	1.3	4.1	5.6	1.6	4.3
Central and Eastern Europe	5.4	2.9	-3.7	0.8	3.0	-5.0	1.0	3.0	-5.0	1.8	3.1	-4.3	2.0
Commonwealth of Independent States	8.6	5.5	-5.1	1.2	5.5	-5.8	2.0	5.5	-6.7	2.1	5.5	-7.5	3.8
Russian Federation	8.1	5.6	-6.0	0.5	5.6	-6.5	1.5	5.6	-7.5	1.5	5.6	-9.0	3.6
Excluding Russian Federation	9.9	5.3	-2.9	3.1	5.4	-3.9	3.2	5.4	-4.7	3.6	5.3	-3.9	4.3
Developing Asia	10.6	7.7	4.8	6.1	7.6	5.5	7.0	7.6	6.2	7.3	7.9	6.5	8.4
China	13.0	9.0	6.5	7.5	9.0	7.5	8.5	9.0	8.5	9.0	9.6	8.7	10.0
India	9.3	7.3	4.5	5.6	7.3	5.4	6.5	7.3	5.4	6.4	7.3	5.6	7.7
ASEAN-5	6.3	4.9	0.0	2.3	4.8	-0.3	3.7	4.8	0.7	4.0	4.7	1.3	4.7
Middle East	6.3	5.9	2.5	3.5	5.2	2.0	3.7	5.4	2.0	4.2	5.3	2.2	4.5
Western hemisphere	5.7	4.2	-1.5	1.6	4.2	-2.6	2.3	4.2	-2.5	2.9	4.2	-2.3	3.7
Brazil	5.7	5.1	-1.3	2.2	5.1	-1.3	2.5	5.1	-0.7	3.5	5.1	-0.4	4.7
Mexico	3.3	1.3	-3.7	1.0	1.3	-7.3	3.0	1.3	-7.3	3.3	1.3	-6.8	4.0
Memorandum													
European Union	3.1	1.1	-4.0	-0.3	1.1	-4.7	-0.1	1.0	-4.2	0.5	1.0	-4.0	1.0
World growth based on market exchange rates	3.8	2.1	-2.5	1.0	2.0	-2.6	1.7	1.8	-2.3	2.3	1.8	-2.1	3.0
World trade volume (goods and services)	7.2	3.3	-11.0	0.6	2.9	-12.2	1.0	3.0	-11.9	2.5	2.8	-12.3	5.8
Imports													
Advanced economies	4.7	0.4	-12.1	0.4	0.4	-13.6	0.6	0.5	-13.7	1.2	0.5	-12.2	5.5
Emerging and developing economies	14.0	10.9	-8.8	0.6	9.4	-9.6	0.8	9.4	-9.5	4.6	8.9	-13.5	6.5
Exports													
Advanced economies	6.1	1.8	-13.5	0.5	2.0	-15.0	1.3	1.9	-13.6	2.0	1.8	-12.1	5.9
Emerging and developing economies	9.5	6.0	-6.4	1.2	4.1	-6.5	1.4	4.6	-7.2	3.6	4.4	-11.7	5.4

Source: IMF World Economic Outlook (various).

Notes: Real effective exchange rates are assumed to remain constant at the levels prevailing prior to projection. Country weights used to construct aggregate growth rates for groups of countries were revised.

[1] The quarterly estimates and projections account for 90 percent of the world purchasing-power-parity weights.

[2] The quarterly estimates and projections account for approximately 77 percent of the emerging and developing economies.

Germany, both posted growth of 0.3 per cent in the second quarter of 2009, after suffering five consecutive quarters of negative growth. By contrast, the British economy shrank by 0.3 per cent and euro zone growth declined to 0.1 per cent. For 2010, forecasts released by the European Commission in October 2009 suggested a modest increase of 0.7 per cent in the GDP of the 27-member European Union.

However, Eastern Europe continued to witness an economic slowdown. In October 2009, the European Bank for Reconstruction and Development (EBRD) forecast that the contraction of the region's economy would be worse than it had foreseen six months ago (6.3% decline compared with a previous forecast of 5.2%). However, growth in 2010 was foreseen to be higher at 2.5 per cent, up from the previously suggested 1.5 per cent, although the upturn was expected to remain fragile (EBRD, 2009).

By the second quarter of 2009, the situation in Asia looked more promising, although some countries were still failing to rebound. Contradicting its earlier predictions, the Asian Development Bank (ADB) said in September 2009 that developing Asia would post stronger growth of 3.9 per cent that year. The projection for 2010 was raised to 6.4 per cent from the 6 per cent predicted earlier, with China and India leading the way. (In March 2009, ADB lowered its 2009 growth forecast for the region to 3.4%, from 5.8% in December 2008 and 7.2% in September 2008).

According to ADB, China was likely to grow by 8.2 per cent in 2009 and by 8.9 per cent in 2010, on condition of a moderate recovery in the global economy and the continuation of the country's fiscal stimulus programme. India was forecast to grow by 6 per cent in 2009 and by 7 per cent in 2010, up from forecasts of 5 per cent and 6.5 per cent, respectively, in March 2009. The Indian economy, as a matter of fact, grew by 7.9 per cent year-on-year, according to official figures released in November 2009 (*Financial Times*, 2009ag), while the Chinese economy posted annualized double-digit growth in the second quarter of 2009.

In November 2009, the OECD predicted modest recovery, with real GDP growing by 1.9 per cent in 2010 in its member countries. It also foresaw a slightly less severe economic contraction for 2009 than it had suggested earlier in September for Europe, the United States and Japan. The aggregate GDP was expected to decline by 3.7 per cent, compared with an earlier forecast of a 4.1 per cent contraction. These were roughly in line with IMF's October 2009 projections.

However, the optimism generated by these trends towards positive growth in the United States and the euro zone was not shared by all. Many analysts were concerned about the underlying weaknesses in these economies and were doubtful about the sustainability of the upbeat signs of economic growth. They said that random figures for a quarter or two do not make a trend, just as Aristotle said that "one swallow does not make a summer" (this is further discussed later in this chapter, in the *"The road to recovery"* section).

Global economic links: Trade, capital flow, aid and remittances

Economic links between countries through trade, capital flows, development aid and migrants' remittances keep the present-day world economy moving. When they dry up, the economy loses steam and slows down. The downturn in these vital economic flows, coupled with an erosion of confidence in the financial system, thus sent ominous signals that the crisis may be deepening.

For more than the past 30 years, international trade has grown two to three times faster than output. It has been an engine of growth and a source of world prosperity, while raising millions of people out of poverty. However, the tide was turning fast. In March 2009, the World Trade Organization (WTO) announced a likely decline of 9 per cent in world merchandise trade (in terms of volume), the biggest contraction since the Second World War. As demand sagged and production fell, the WTO forecast a 10 per cent decline in exports for advanced economies and a 2–3 per cent decline for developing-country economies. However, later figures for global trade looked even more ominous, suggesting a sharper fall of nearly 12 per cent for 2009 (*Financial Times*, 2009o).[3] During the previous three recessions mentioned earlier (see Table 1), world trade had remained stagnant.

As the recession began to take hold in the fourth quarter of 2008, marked by a sharp downturn in trade, the WTO noted in March 2009 that little had changed to give ground for optimism. Countries that had been powerhouses for export – Germany, China and Japan – faced a sharp downturn in trade, as their trading partners continued to be mired in recession. Germany's exports fell by 20 per cent in February 2009 compared to 2008 figures, while Japan's plunged by 46 per cent.

It was feared that China, which was heavily dependent on exports, could face a contraction of 0.6 per cent in its GDP for every 1 per cent fall in its exports.

[3] As of August 2009, however, the WTO was sticking to its earlier forecast of a 10 per cent drop in merchandise trade volume for 2009.

In February 2009, the country's exports fell by 25 per cent from February 2008 figures; imports declined by 24 per cent after dropping 43 per cent in January. The trend was similar in Taiwan Province of China and in most other parts of Asia. For Taiwan Province of China and the Philippines, exports were barely more than half of what they had been in 2008. The Republic of Korea, another country heavily dependent on trade, reported a record 33 per cent fall in exports in January 2009. In the same month, Indonesia announced a 36 per cent fall in exports, exceeding Thailand's 25 per cent decline. Total exports for five of Latin America's larger economies fell by a third in the last five months of 2008, and there were few signs of significant recovery. In November 2008, the euro zone saw its biggest monthly fall in exports in eight years: exports declined by 4.7 per cent month-on-month, extending a 2.8 per cent fall in October.

Increased earnings from commodity exports had helped many African countries to boost growth, opening up prospects for a better future. However, with a sharp decline in both volume and prices, these countries faced serious difficulty. American imports from middle-income countries fell 3 per cent in the year to November 2008, but imports from sub-Saharan Africa declined 12 per cent.

Policy trends in countries did not make the outlook any more reassuring. In November 2008, the G20 made a commitment to shun trade protectionism, a commitment that it reiterated at its April 2009 meeting in London. However, by that time, at least 17 countries in the group had already used a total of 47 protectionist measures. By September 2009, 20 major economies may have been responsible for as many as 121 "blatantly protectionist" measures, with 134 more in the pipeline, according to an analysis by Global Trade Alert, an international trade monitoring service. Governments had reaffirmed their commitment not to provide subsidies for exports, but they tended to act differently. In reality, on average, a G20 member country had broken the non-protectionism pledge once every three days in the year since the group's November 2008 meeting in Washington, D.C., according to Simon Evenett, coordinator of Global Trade Alert.

In September 2009, several international agencies warned that incremental protectionism risked throwing "sand in the gears" of international trade at a time when rising unemployment would continue to fuel protectionist pressures "for years to come" (*Financial Times*, 2009u). The WTO recorded 83 trade-restricting measures undertaken by 24 countries during the second quarter of 2009 – more than double the number of trade-liberalizing measures enacted during the same period. Although the WTO report noted that the worst abuses had largely been contained, it warned that a surge of new anti-dumping investigations could emerge as the economic crisis dragged on.

Unlike in the 1930s, when many governments raised trade barriers across the board mostly by raising tariffs, trade-distorting protectionist measures in 2009 (e.g. the use of safeguard measures without proving unfair pricing) were more subtle and less visible. According to the WTO, the number of such measures increased from two to 16 in the first seven months of 2009 compared with the previous year, as state aid for troubled industries such as automobiles significantly increased. According to Global Trade Alert, since November 2008, G20 governments had announced twice as many trade-distorting government bailouts as increases in tariffs in troubled industries.

In the United States, the "Buy American" provision in the 2009 stimulus bill, though watered down to make it compatible with US treaty obligations, still required that only US-made steel and concrete be used in infrastructure projects. Also, cities and some states in the United States were not bound by US trade treaty obligations (*The New York Times*, 2009d).

It is interesting to note that a study by Jeffery Schott and Gary Clyde Hufbauer of the Washington, D.C.-based Peterson Institute for International Economics estimated that the "Buy American" provision could "save" 9,000 American jobs, compared with the 650,000 jobs supported by foreign-government procurement of American exports. This can be jeopardized in case of retaliation, and there were already signs of this. For example, according to newspaper reports, after Canadian companies were barred from bidding for American procurement, some 12 Canadian cities passed ordinances against buying American. At the same time, some US-based companies, such as Duferco Farrell in Pennsylvania, cut jobs after losing their customers, because some of their goods were partly produced abroad. In a slightly different situation, the Westlake Chemical Corporation in Houston lost sales to a Canadian vinyl pipe maker that cut back production because it was prevented from bidding for some American contracts.

Although there was no large-scale trade war across sectors, it was feared that the US decision to impose a 35 per cent tariff on Chinese tyres could further fuel protectionist trends. In France, car makers were asked to buy domestic components and repatriate production back home in return for state aid of EUR 6 billion; in Spain, consumers were urged to buy home-spun goods. The planned German aid to smooth the sale of Opel and Vauxhall (which was subsequently overtaken by events) raised concerns elsewhere in Europe, especially in the UK. Neelie Kroes, then EU competition commissioner, warned member states against "stealing jobs" from other countries by "bribing", an act that risked sparking a trade war (*Financial Times*, 2009v).

Some were worried that the world might see the return of the Smooth–Hawley US tariff laws that drove the 1929 US stock market meltdown into the

Great Depression of the early 1930s. This may have been an alarmist view. The imposition of US import tariffs on Chinese steel pipes and car tyres and the Chinese counter-attacks on US poultry and auto parts, for example, were minor trade spats and were therefore unlikely to spark a full-fledged trade war. Furthermore, China's restrictions on its own exports of raw materials – which, in effect, drive down the prices set by domestic companies – had not been a major source of conflict. Also, on the whole, trade protectionism, as already mentioned, had not been a hallmark of the 2008–2009 crisis. As this study was being prepared, a report on new trade restrictions commissioned by the G20 governments was released. It confirmed that the expected surge of protectionism following the crisis has not materialized.

Indeed, by the second half of 2009, trade had begun to increase, and there seemed to be no permanent damage to the existing structure of trade relationships. A number of countries were able to make impressive gains in external trade. For China, the increase was spectacular, owing largely to aggressive stimulus programmes. China's external trade rose by 17.7 per cent in December 2009 compared with the year before, and the country emerged as the world's largest exporter. Although trade imbalance continued to be a nagging problem, the United States made some significant gains in its export trade as well. Overall, global trade in goods rose fast, and monthly figures increased to as high as 4.8 per cent in December 2009. On 26 March 2010, the WTO forecast a 9.5 per cent expansion in global trade in 2010.

However, these increases were relative to the very low base figures of 2009. Economists and exporters were still wary about the sustainability of these gains. As of January 2010, while China, for example, was making strides towards recovery, there were reports that in Zhejiang, a main exporting province in eastern China, only 28 per cent of export companies had at least three months of orders on their books, which were still insufficient for a stable level of production and demand, according to Zhou Bijian, a Zhejiang provincial government official (*Financial Times*, 2010a). At the same time, there were concerns about an overheating economy and potential inflation.

There is little doubt that if recovery remained weak or the economy worsened and job losses continued, governments may give in to populist pressures to protect jobs at home by erecting trade barriers in many different forms and guises, though this will only worsen the situation.

As regards the study commissioned by G20 governments (referred to earlier), critics have indeed argued that it did not fully capture the extent of so-called murky protectionism or less-obvious protectionist measures such as financial and industry bailouts. As Simon Evenett, coordinator of Global Trade Alert, said: "Protectionism in 2009 may not have hit 1930s levels, but it was well above trend in almost every major trading nation" (*Financial Times*, 2010c).

Admittedly, given the signs of recovery, a breakdown of the world trading system did not seem very likely, but the risk could stem from another source. A surge of cheap imports, largely one-sided flows from export-led countries such as China, could trigger countermeasures from trading partners. The EU, for example, was already concerned that in the absence of trade flows in both directions, there could be a protectionist backlash with a dangerous snowball effect (*Financial Times*, 2009af). The weakening of the euro changed the situation somewhat. However, in the United States, political pressure was building to impose new import restrictions against "unfair exchange rates." This highlights the importance of ensuring a more balanced growth of the world economy.

Some analysts were in fact concerned about the looming signs of trade protectionism through competitive currency devaluation. Viet Nam's decision in November 2009 to devalue its currency by 5 per cent to protect itself from the undervaluation of the Chinese renminbi and the worried response from Thailand and other Asian countries added to this fear (*Financial Times*, 2009ah). In such a situation, countries which are not in a position, or are unwilling, to devalue their currencies may well be tempted to take recourse to direct and indirect forms of trade protection to defend their trade balance, as had happened both during and prior to the Great Depression of the 1930s.

According to some economists, there was yet another source of potential danger for countries. The use of fiscal stimulus to fight the recession is likely to lead to an increase in public debt; it may also encourage additional imports and thus increase import bills, while free-riding trade partners benefit from increased demand for their exports. Should this happen, countries using large-scale fiscal stimulus may well be inclined to take protectionist measures against foreign imports, unless countries coordinate their policy measures (Eichengreen and Irwin, 2009a, 2009b).

Trade finance and capital flows: Although a significant part of international trade has been taking place as intra-firm transactions in recent years, a fifth of the USD 15,000 billion in trade flows is believed to have been financed by letters of credit, creating a market of USD 3,000 billion. The depletion of funds available in this market – a shortfall of between USD 100 billion and USD 300 billion, according to WTO experts – is considered an important factor in the overall decline in trade.

The high, though declining, cost and long maturity of trade finance also constrained its use. Banks that accept state aid came under pressure to think along national lines and withdraw from lending outside their home markets. Although figures showing partial trade recovery at the end of 2009 seemed to suggest that the importance initially attached to trade finance as a cause of its decline may have been overrated, there is little doubt that it did play a part, at least for some time, in constraining trade. In fact, failure to secure trade financing, coupled with high food prices, led several developing countries, including Malaysia, Morocco, the Russian Federation and Viet Nam, to rely on intergovernmental barter deals to trade in commodities ranging from rice to vegetable oil (*Financial Times*, 2009b).

Lack of trade finance was not the only problem; other financial flows were also drying up. A flight to safety and rising home bias, often encouraged by governments, led to a sharp contraction of gross global capital flows. As financial protectionism gained ground, cross-border bank lending even within the OECD area badly suffered (*Financial Times*, 2009e).[4] Net private flows to emerging and developing countries nearly collapsed. Their currencies (except those pegged to the US dollar) weakened sharply, despite resort to international reserves for support.

In March 2009, the World Bank estimated that developing countries were facing a financing gap of USD 270 billion to USD 700 billion a year as capital flows slowed down. The Washington, D.C.-based International Institute of Finance thought private capital flows to emerging economies would probably slump from almost USD 1 trillion in 2007 to USD 165 billion in 2009. The Institute forecast that capital flow to Latin America would fall by more than half to USD 43 billion in 2009 compared to 2008 figures, and would be significantly down from USD 184 billion in 2007. As new democracies with fledgling market economies and heavy dependence on foreign credit, countries in Central and Eastern Europe faced a fragile financial situation. In April 2009, the IMF estimated that the region's financing gap – the money that cannot be found in the market – could be USD 123 billion in 2009 and USD 63 billion in 2010.[5] The Fund added that this figure could be even higher if the decline in growth exceeded 2.5 per cent in 2009. For Asia, in May 2009, Haruhiko Kuroda, president of ADB, expressed his concern by suggesting that "almost all developing member countries now have funding problems." The risk premiums were so high, he added, that it would be almost impossible for developing member countries to borrow from capital markets, except for

[4] As Richard Lambert, director general of the Confederation of British Industry, remarked, international banks used to account for 40 per cent of lending in the UK. "They have now gone, and that's why we have a funding problem and a credit crunch."

[5] This was based on the assumption that the region's debt rollover rates declined to 50 per cent for private debt and 90 per cent for sovereign debt in 2009, with modest improvements in 2010.

China.[6] As for Africa, the African Development Bank was worried that the region's current accounts, in surplus of GDP by 3.8 per cent in 2007, would show a 6 per cent deficit in 2009.

Foreign direct investment (FDI), an important component of global capital flows, was foreseen to take a plunge from USD 1.7 trillion in 2008 to USD 1.2 trillion in 2009, a decline of more than 29 per cent, according to the United Nations Conference on Trade and Development (UNCTAD, 2009). The organization also declared that "the crisis has changed the FDI landscape," adding that such a fall would take FDI to levels seen five years ago. In 2008, FDI was already short by 14 per cent from its historic peak of USD 1.98 trillion in 2007. However, the FDI in developing economies actually rose in 2008, with record inflows to Africa and countries in Asia, although inflows to rich countries slowed down. However, things changed in 2009 for both groups of countries: with some rare exceptions, such as inflows to the UK (which rose by 17.6% to USD 63.2 billion in the first three months of 2009), FDI fell across rich and poor countries.

In the first quarter of 2009, FDI inflows to the United States declined by 42 per cent to USD 33.3 billion, while inflows to the EU fell by 43 per cent to USD 109.5 billion. In developing regions, inflows to India declined by a dramatic 56 per cent in the first quarter of 2009; China's fell by 21 per cent; and Brazil's declined by 39 per cent. In Africa, after reaching a record USD 88 billion in 2008, inflows dropped by as much as 67 per cent in 2009. Nearly 85 per cent of the 240 transnational companies surveyed for the UNCTAD report said the recession influenced their decision to cut FDI.

In its report, UNCTAD forecast slow recovery worldwide – to over USD 1.4 trillion in 2010 and USD 1.8 trillion in 2011. However, it warned that "a more restrictive" approach was developing in some countries, with "growing evidence of covert protectionism." If this approach gained further ground, the situation could worsen, the organization added. Also, the decline in cross-border equity investment – as opposed to reinvested earnings or intra-company loans – was likely to be slower than in previous downturns.

Sub-Saharan countries raised USD 6.5 billion in international bonds in 2007; in 2008, they raised nothing. Ghana, Kenya, the United Republic of Tanzania and Uganda all shelved their euro bond issues, as did Nigeria for the naira-denominated bond issue it had planned earlier. Many developing countries were worried that the huge stock of public debt held by rich countries would

[6] The ADB estimated that the capital losses in 2008 of Asian countries, excluding Japan, were over USD 9.6 trillion (109% of GDP), compared with losses of USD 2.1 trillion (57% of GDP) for Latin America, and a global average of 80–85 per cent of GDP. It estimated that the decline in the value of financial assets worldwide reached more than USD 50 trillion in 2008.

crowd them out as borrowers in the capital market. World Bank president Robert Zoellick echoed this concern by saying that "the banking bailouts and stimulus spending by the rich world were crowding out emerging markets... and made [it] harder for developing countries to issue bonds" (*Financial Times*, 2009c).

In September 2009, the World Bank suggested that the global economic crisis threatened to wipe out steady improvements made in the public finances of many poor countries between 2000 and 2007. An estimated 43 of the poorest countries faced a core spending gap of USD 11.6 billion in 2009. Some in this group would be unable to fund fiscal deficits and would thus have to cut spending in critical sectors such as health, education and infrastructure. Unable to follow the rich world's lead to kick-start their economies by using fiscal stimulus, many of these poor countries would be left behind on the way to recovery (*Financial Times*, 2009t; World Bank, 2009b).

Development aid: For many poor countries, aid is another important source of external financial support. As World Bank research, backed by other studies and empirical evidence, has shown, when well planned and effectively used, aid, alongside policy reform, can be of much help to resource-short countries in alleviating poverty and promoting development. In the wake of the crisis, aid gained additional importance for a number of poor countries as they faced a fall in income from such other sources as tourism, exports, capital inflows and migrants' remittances. While it is true that in the past, aid funds had gone down the rathole, often due to the fault of both donors and recipients, this time, things could be different for several reasons:

First, the limitations and potential pitfalls of aid are now better understood by both donors (including aid agencies) and recipients. Increased public vigilance over the planning and use of aid and the active participation of the private sector and non-governmental organizations (NGOs) in the process are also part of the new reality.

Second, the present global crisis has sharpened political sensitivity in almost every country over any misuse of public funds, especially through corrupt practices or ostentatious projects for the benefit of a few. There are no doubt many ways in which aid performance can be improved and pitfalls avoided. However, as Duncan Green, head of research at Oxfam, a UK-based charity, said, this must not be "a smokescreen for rich governments to cut aid in the middle of a global recession."

With new guidelines and special safeguards against abuse, aid can be particularly useful to poor countries, especially those that are heavily dependent on migrants' remittances, as they face the fallout of the recession.

However, the flow of aid was falling behind the commitment made by rich countries at Gleneagles in 2005. Although aid for 2008 showed an increase to about USD 120 billion, there was still a shortfall of USD 25 billion a year in reaching the Gleneagles targets by 2010; in addition, several countries had relied on "front loading" (i.e. drawing on funds from future budgets to make their contributions). The OECD feared the pledge might well be revoked as the economic crisis put pressure on aid. Further, little was known at the time of writing about a pledge of USD 20 billion made by the Group of Eight (G8) meeting in Italy for agricultural development. Many analysts feared that, instead of new money, the pledge was likely to be mostly a repackaging of old commitments under bilateral aid programmes. As Robert Zoellick, the World Bank president, picturesquely remarked: "Paper pledges alone will not put seeds in soil or feed the hungry."

As a share of income, the aid contribution of OECD countries in 2008 amounted to 0.3 per cent, up from 0.28 per cent in 2007. However, this only brought aid levels back to those seen in 1993. Between 1992 and 1997, in a much weaker global economic downturn, aid fell from 0.33 per cent to 0.22 per cent of national income. Further, since aid contribution is generally committed and assessed as a percentage of national income, the falling GDP of donor countries could also imply a smaller amount of actual aid.

An encouraging development amid rising concerns that the EU was failing to live up to its international commitments was that, in April 2010, policymakers decided to urge member states to consider laws that would make development aid a protected or non-discretionary item in their national budgets. Such laws were already in place in Belgium and were under consideration in the UK.

As in many previous economic downturns, private donation was declining as well. True, the Gates Foundation, for example, was to increase its spending to USD 3.8 billion in 2009 from USD 3.3 billion in the previous year to "set an example" for Western governments, as Bill Gates put it in February 2009. However, even the Gates Foundation was not immune from the financial turmoil. The increase in the Foundation's giving in 2009 was less than what it had originally planned. As Jeff Raikes, the Foundation's chief executive officer, wrote in November 2008: "The financial crisis is affecting everyone, from our foundation to our partners" (*The Wall Street Journal*, 2008). In November 2008, the International Federation of Red Cross and Red Crescent Societies, the world's biggest humanitarian organization, was considering cutting staff and shelving projects as it faced slashing of aid contributions by recession-hit donors (*Financial Times*, 2008b).

While economic woes were increasing demand for the services of private charities, especially those related to poverty relief, the recession was making severe dents in both the income and assets of charity-supporting foundations. In the United States, the Foundation Center found that US charitable foundations lost USD 150 billion in 2008. Paul Light, a professor of public service at New York University, predicted that 100,000 non-profit organizations in the United States that depended largely on foundations for their funding would disappear. In the UK, according to the Charities Commission, 64 per cent of charities with an annual income of over GBP 1 million were concerned that their resources or funding might be greatly affected.

Migrants' remittances: Remittances to developing countries, which increased sharply from USD 228 billion in 2006 to USD 338 billion in 2008, have emerged as an important source of external finance for a number of these countries (Ratha et al., 2009a, 2009b) (see Table 3 in chapter 3). However, with the recession gaining ground, the combined effects of declines in both new immigration flows and migrant stocks, coupled with the spread of joblessness and a decline in the earnings of migrants and a growing feeling of economic uncertainty among them, led to a deceleration in the flows of remittances. An increase in the share of non-working-age migrants in new flows to a number of OECD countries and the lower employment outcome of many of those who entered though non-labour migration channels (discussed in chapter 3) were also having a depressive effect on remittances. The World Bank's earlier forecast of a likely decline in remittances of just 1 per cent for 2009 was revised and updated in July 2009 to suggest a decline of between 7.3 per cent and 10 per cent in the same year and a small improvement for 2010. In November 2009, the World Bank again revised these figures to suggest a slightly less pessimistic scenario: a decline of 6.1 per cent for 2009 and a small increase of 1.4 per cent for 2010.

The decline in remittance flows was particularly disturbing for poor countries where remittances accounted for a high percentage of GDP. In over 20 countries, remittances accounted for 10 per cent of GDP, and in countries such as Tajikistan, Tonga and the Republic of Moldova, for more than 30 per cent of GDP. In several regions, remittance declines were highly concentrated in precisely these countries (this is further discussed in the section on *"Remittances"* in chapter 3).

1.3 Joblessness, poverty and economic insecurity: Possible derailment of the Millennium Development Goals (MDG) anti-poverty time table?

The economic downturn was taking a heavy toll on job markets in both rich and poor countries. In March 2009, the International Labour Organization

(ILO) envisaged that worldwide unemployment could increase by at least 38 million by the end of 2009, driving the global unemployment rate to 7 per cent at a minimum (ILO, 2009). Nearly 90 million additional people were estimated to join the labour force between 2009 and 2010, putting further pressure on job markets. In January 2010, ILO reaffirmed that global unemployment hit a record high in 2009 and that it was likely to remain high in 2010. The number of jobless persons soared since the end of 2007 to reach 212 million.

In 2007, the unemployment rate in OECD countries fell to a 25-year low of 5.5 per cent, but as the recession took hold, the situation changed rapidly. In March 2009, the OECD estimated that the unemployment rate in its 30 member countries could reach 10 per cent, involving 25 million people, by the end of 2010. Angel Gurria, the head of the OECD, described it as "by far the largest and most rapid increase in OECD unemployment in the post-war period" that could turn the downturn into a "jobs and social crisis." The number of people on the dole in G7 nations was expected to double from levels seen in mid-2007, reaching about 36 million people in mid-2010. In November 2009, the OECD warned that, despite the modest economic recovery, unemployment in the rich world was set to continue to rise well into 2010 and to fall modestly in the following year from a peak of more than 9 per cent of the labour force.

The unemployment rate in the United States reached 8.9 per cent in April 2009 and 9.4 per cent (a total of 14.5 million people unemployed) in May 2009. The unemployment rate was 10 per cent in 14 US states and the District of Columbia in August (as was foreseen for the country by the OECD as well as by the US government as a worst-case economic scenario during its recent bank stress exercise).[7] By September 2009, joblessness had already edged up to 9.8 per cent, and by the end of October, to 10.2 per cent, bringing the number of jobs lost to 7.3 million since December 2007.

According to the US Department of Labor, during the 2001 recession, the number of jobs lost slightly exceeded the number of job openings. In contrast, at the beginning of 2009, the ratio was a little more than 2 to 1, and by September 2009, it jumped to 6 to 1. The pace of increase in unemployment in 48 US states was unprecedented in the post-war period. As of September 2009, the number of people officially unemployed – 15.1 million – was greater than the population of 46 out of 50 US states.

---

[7] The US administration's own economic projection – which took into account the additional jobs its new policies were expected to create – was that unemployment, which was below 5 per cent in 2007, would average 9.8 per cent in 2010, 8.6 per cent in 2011 and 7.7 per cent in 2012.

The number of part-time workers, which is not reflected in the headline unemployment rate, rose by almost 80 per cent to a record high of 8.6 million in the 12 months to February 2009. If these part-time workers, as well as those who wanted full-time employment but could only get part-time jobs, were included, the percentage of the unemployed, according to the US Department of Labor, would have been 17.5 per cent – or one in six – at the end of October 2009.[8] The unemployment rate would have been higher if all those who dropped out of the workforce out of despair (estimated at 570,000 people in August 2009) were included. The oft-quoted job loss data also failed to take into account the 1 million people who once worked in residential construction or new jobseekers – some 2.8 million during the recession – such as school and college graduates, stay-at-home-parents, including retired persons, who wanted to go back to work. If the short-shift work system, under which working hours and wages were reduced (further discussed later in this chapter and also in chapter 4), were not in operation, the same work would probably be done in a normal work week with 3.5 million fewer staff, driving the unemployment rate by another 2.5 per cent.

Some analysts (e.g. ING chief economist Rob Carnell) forecast that the unemployment rate would reach 11 per cent or higher by the middle of 2010 before it starts to head down (*Financial Times*, 2009p). In November 2009, Charles Evans, the president of the Federal Reserve Bank of Chicago, thought that the US unemployment rate might peak at about 10.5 per cent in the spring of 2010, and fall to about 9.5 per cent by the end of 2010 (*Financial Times*, 2009ad). The net loss of 85,000 jobs in December 2009, although a significant improvement over the situation for much of the year, indicated employers' continued resistance to hiring new workers, especially on a permanent basis.

In the euro zone, joblessness reached 9.7 per cent in September 2009, compared with 7.7 per cent in the same period in 2008, and was expected to reach 11 per cent in 2010. In the EU-27, the unemployment rate jumped from 7.1 per cent in September 2008 to 9.2 per cent in September 2009. A total of more than 22 million men and women in the EU-27 were unemployed in September 2009, of which over 15 million were in the euro area. In Spain, unemployment reached 19.3 per cent, the highest level in more than 12 years. Youth unemployment in the euro area was 20.1 per cent in September 2009, compared with 15.7 per cent in 2008 (Eurostat, 2009). During the same period, the unemployment rate increased in all EU member states.

[8] This refers to the broadest measure, the so-called U6 as distinct from the so-called U3 number that includes only those out of work who are still looking for jobs.

Germany saw a small rise in its unemployment rate from 7.1 per cent to 7.6 per cent. However, given the country's excess industrial capacity, further downsizing of the labour market looked most likely. Between the second quarters of 2008 and 2009, unemployment rates rose from 8.1 per cent to 19.7 per cent in Latvia and from 4.1 per cent to 13.3 per cent in Estonia. In the UK, the number of unemployment benefit claimants per vacancy more than doubled between 2008 and 2009 to an average of 10, according to the British Trades Union Congress. Unemployment in some euro zone countries, notably Germany, was less severe than expected as government-subsidized short-time working schemes made it possible for companies to cut working hours instead of jobs.

According to an ILO estimate, based on media reports, European companies shed 350,000 jobs, compared with 640,000 jobs by US companies, in the first half of 2009. Some analysts believed that deeper job cuts by US companies were the reason why they were performing better than companies in the euro zone. However, this move could also have a short-term negative effect on the economy as a whole, as massive cuts in jobs could destroy confidence in the economy as well as in the company, retarding economic recovery. Although Europe typically lags behind the United States, job losses continued to mount there as well, and unemployment in both Europe and the United States reached 10 per cent in November 2009.

The situation was no less grim elsewhere. Even some of the erstwhile fastest-growing countries were unable to escape the ravages of the economic crisis. In December 2008, a Chinese official was quoted as saying that 10 million people had been laid off so far due to the crisis, and several officials had warned of the risk of social unrest if unemployment rose any further (*Financial Times*, 2009a). In a similar vein, in January 2009 an article in a magazine published by the official Xinhua News Agency cautioned: "Without doubt, we are now entering a peak period for mass incidents" (Xinhua News, 2009). At a cabinet meeting in the same month, Chinese Premier Wen Jiabao reportedly said that "the country's employment (situation) is extremely grim" (*New York Times*, 2009b). In March 2009, according to the National Statistics Bureau, half of China's 140 million internal migrants returned to their villages for the New Year; of this number, 14 million remained in their villages and 11 million were jobless in cities (Migration News, 2009b).

Another report, based on a survey by the agriculture ministry, put the unemployment figure at more than 20 million for rural internal migrants who returned home jobless as a result of the crisis (excluding those who remained in cities after having been made redundant) (*Financial Times*, 2009d).[9] As of February 2009, India was estimated to have lost half a million jobs in the export-related sector due to the recession. In the Republic of Korea, the number of unemployed rose to 924,000 in February 2009, up 13 per cent compared with the same month in 2008. South Africa was set to lose a quarter of a million of jobs, undermining government plans to cut the unemployment rate to 14 per cent by 2014.

A December 2009 report based on a survey of 35 countries by Manpower, a UK-based recruitment agency, saw a glimmer of hope. Employers in 25 of these countries expected net hiring in 2010 (Manpower, 2009). According to the report, employers in the Asia-Pacific region were expecting hiring to return to its pre-recession pace. While the global market remained difficult, in the Americas and Europe, there were limited but continued positive signals. A separate survey of 34 countries by Antal, another employment agency, found that job prospects for professionals and managers were improving for the first time since autumn 2008 (Antal International, 2009).

Too much optimism over these findings, however, seemed misplaced at least for three reasons. While hiring intentions in Asia were quite buoyant, this did not include Japan. US employers were still reluctant to start taking on staff again except on a temporary basis. Euro zone job markets were sluggish, with four fifths of employers across Europe expecting no changes in staff and Spain, Ireland and Romania anticipating declines. Second, the surveys were limited to selected firms in the organized sector and did not include some of the worst-affected sectors. Third, and most important, even if the improvements shown in the survey results truly marked a turning point in terms of the end of job losses and some new recruitment, this was still a long way off from the pre-recession level of employment (this is further discussed in the last section of this chapter).

When joblessness and poverty go hand in hand

Poverty: Rising unemployment and downward pressure on earnings in the informal sector and in other vulnerable or precarious jobs, triggered or exacerbated by the recession, seriously aggravated global poverty. The lack of adequate social safety nets in many poor countries, especially those heavily dependent on remittances, made the situation worse.

In January 2009, the ILO projected that between 40 per cent and 50 per cent of men and women globally would be unable to earn enough

[9] In an interview given to the *Financial Times* on 1 February 2009, Mr Wen Jiabao, the Chinese premier, used a much lower figure of 12 million.

to lift themselves and their families out of the poverty line of USD 2 a day in 2009 (ILO, 2009).[10] An increase in vulnerable or precarious jobs would be a major contributing factor in raising the number of the working poor (see Figure 1).

The World Bank estimated that a 1 per cent decline in growth will drive an additional 20 million people to poverty in developing countries. It suggested that a total of 65 million additional people were likely to fall below the poverty line of USD 2 a day in 2009; of this figure, 45 million people were already living below the poverty line as of April 2009.[11] In September 2009, the World Bank further suggested that, by the end of 2010, the global economic crisis would push almost 90 million additional people into extreme poverty.

Figure 1: Increase in vulnerable employment and working poor (in millions; change from 2007 to 2009)

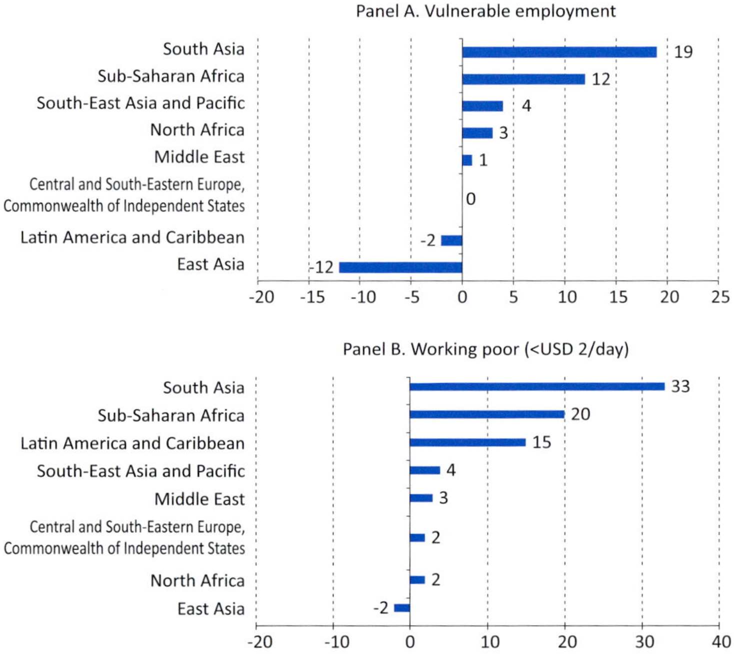

Source: ILO, 2009.

[10] The estimate was based on the worst-case scenario for economic growth in 2009.

[11] The number mentioned by World Bank president Robert Zoellick at the time of the April 2009 G20 summit in London was 65 million.

The rise in food prices between 2005 and 2008 further aggravated human hardship, since the poor in developing countries spend a disproportionately high proportion (50% or more) of their income on food. It thus increased the share of the population of several regions in extreme poverty by 1 per cent, derailing progress towards MDGs. Over 35 years have elapsed since Henry Kissinger, then US Secretary of State, told the first World Food Conference in 1974 that no child on earth would go to bed hungry within 10 years. Today, 1 billion people do exactly that, and every six seconds, a child dies out of hunger-related causes. Significantly, at the summit on food security held in Rome in November 2009, the proposal to set a timeline for the eradication of hunger was taken off the pledge (*Financial Times*, 2009y).

South Asia, the Middle East and East Asia suffered the most from the hike in food prices, which sparked food riots in countries ranging from Bangladesh to Haiti. In India, a poor monsoon and a faltering agriculture sector, set against the backdrop of the global economic crisis, led to food shortages and a surge in food prices, leading to increased industrial strikes and prompting the authorities to launch countrywide raids on food hoarders. According to some analysts, a poor monsoon and a 2 per cent fall in agricultural output knocks off 1 percentage point from India's GDP growth (*Financial Times*, 2009n).

In Africa, the impact was less severe, since the rise in food prices was lower than in some other regions. Nevertheless, Africa did not escape the onslaught of poverty propelled by the recession. The UK-based Oxfam, for example, estimated that the average income of the 391 million Africans living on less than USD 1.25 a day was to take a dramatic hit of 20 per cent.

Although food prices had declined since July 2008, they still remained well above levels seen in the 1990s, and many foresee a significant rise in the coming years. As Jacques Diouf, director general of the Food and Agriculture Organization of the United Nations (FAO), crisply warned, given the past neglect of agriculture, global recovery carried new risks of a price surge in food commodities.

Rich countries were not spared. In the United States, for example, the poverty rate climbed from 12.5 per cent in 2007 to 13.2 per cent in 2008, the highest level since 1997; it was expected to rise further in 2009 due to an increase in joblessness (DeNavas-Walt et al., 2009).[12] According to the US Census Bureau, about 40 million US residents in 2009 lived below the poverty line, defined as an income of USD 22,025 for a family of four. The use of food stamps was at a record high: it was already feeding 37 million people (one

[12] Although the accuracy of the US census, which suffers from certain flaws, is open to debate, the data present a good measure of long-term trends.

in eight Americans), including 14 million (one in four) children (Mathematica Policy Research, 2010; *The New York Times*, 2009j, 2010a). This number, which had risen by 46 per cent since 2006, seemed to be climbing. About 6 million people (roughly one in 50) lived in households with a reported income that consisted of nothing but a food stamp card. Already, a third of Hispanic children and more than a third of African American children were living in poverty and analysts at the Washington, D.C.-based Economic Policy Institute thought that without an aggressive new intervention by the federal government, the poverty rate for these children could reach 50 per cent.

Roughly 2.7 million jobless people, many of them already poor, were set to lose their unemployment benefits in the second quarter of 2010 had Congress not approved the US administration's proposal to extend the date of payment. Despite political acrimony and protracted legislative debate, the bill finally went through in July 2010.

Joblessness and inequality: In times of economic crisis, joblessness tends to hit harder those who are already poor. This aggravates the extent and depth of poverty in both rich and poor countries. A significant proportion of migrants belong to these poorer groups. In the United States, recent investigation by the Center for Labor Market Studies at Northeastern University revealed how joblessness and income inequality tend to be closely correlated (Sum and Khatiwada, 2010). The study divided American households into 10 groups based on annual household incomes and then analysed labour conditions in each group during the fourth quarter of 2009. The richest group, with household incomes of USD 150,000 or more, had an unemployment rate of 3.2 per cent during that quarter. The next richest group, with incomes of USD 100,000 to USD 149,999, had an unemployment rate of 4 per cent. By contrast, the poorest group, with incomes of USD 12,499 or less, had an unemployment rate of 30.8 per cent, and the slightly-less-poor group, with incomes of USD 12,500 to USD 20,000, had an unemployment rate of 19.1 per cent.

If the picture looks disquieting, it gets worse when data about underemployment (including part-time workers who would like to work full time and those who have given up looking for jobs but would take a job if available) are taken into account. In the poorest group, the unemployment rate would then jump to 20.6 per cent as against 1.6 per cent for the richest group – a difference of 13 times. The study showed that middle-income groups also suffered, but the worst sufferers were the lower-income groups (Sum and Khatiwada, 2010).

Even before the recession, it had been far from certain that the MDG timetable on poverty alleviation (i.e. halving world poverty by 2015) would be fully met. The recession-induced increase in poverty made the situation even more uncertain and the challenge even more daunting. More so since, as discussed later in this chapter, even in the event that the world economy starts to gain steam in 2010–2011, there would almost inevitably be a significant time gap between output recovery and labour market recovery in terms of jobs and earnings (this is further discussed later in this chapter, in the section *"Time lag between output recovery and employment recovery"*). For the reasons discussed in chapter 3, a high proportion of migrants will continue to be among the worst sufferers.

1.4 The road to recovery

Is global recovery around the corner? What kind of recovery?

As already indicated, since around the middle of 2009, there has been a growing belief among economists and intergovernmental agencies (including the IMF, the European Central Bank (ECB), and the European Commission) that the world economy would likely recover in 2010. However, at the time of writing, there was still no clear consensus on the shape of the recovery or how robust it was likely to be. Opinions remained sharply divided. Since economists are fond of indicating their views on the nature of economic recovery by using the shapes of different alphabets, one analyst jokingly remarked that "soon there won't be enough alphabets left for the economists to play the game."

At one extreme, a number of economists thought that positive output growth in the second quarter of 2009, followed by the gathering pace of manufacturing activity in August in countries such as the United States, China, France and Germany, and the upcoming need for restocking inventories (that had been aggressively de-stocked), were strong evidence of a powerful – and possibly V-shaped – recovery of the world economy. At the other extreme, there were sceptics who saw many clouds looming and felt that these temporary blips did not indicate a trend of sustainable growth. As William White, one of the few economists who had predicted the recession, remarked: "The world has not tackled the problems at the heart of the economic downturn, and is likely to slip back into recession...government actions to help the economy in the short run might be sowing the seeds of future crises" (*Financial Times*, 2009q). "The only thing that would really surprise me is a rapid and sustainable recovery from the position we are in," White added. The economist was in fact predicting a W-shaped recovery, or a so-called double-dip recession (one downturn followed by another on the road to recovery).

Some other economists took a more nuanced view of the situation as they analysed the emerging green roots of growth alongside the brown roots of economic stagnation. In view of the lingering weaknesses in the world economy, they foresaw sluggish or anaemic performance, a U- or L-shaped recovery, with growth remaining below pre-recession trends for at least a couple of years.

A slightly different variation on this view is that, for a few quarters in the future, there could well be a relatively sharp economic upturn as a rebound from the depths of decline, triggered by a variety of financial and fiscal stimulus plans. Some initial signs of this were already discernible in the United States, parts of the euro zone and much of Asia in the second half of 2009. However, according to these analysts, the recovery would then slow down when stimulus packages are withdrawn, and the world economy would still struggle to continue to recover from the ravages of the recession and repair its fiscal deficit.

In other words, according to this view, the *initial* recovery might appear to be relatively sharp but it would soon be followed by a sluggish trend – half of a W-shaped recovery, showing a sharp initial uptake, followed by a straight line mirroring slow growth for several years (the shape of recovery would look more like a square root sign √‾).

In examining the prospects and shape of recovery, the IMF, in its October 2009 *World Economic Outlook*, affirmed that economic growth had turned positive but warned that the process would be slow and sluggish. By suggesting that the "risks to the outlook remain on the downside," IMF lent credence to those taking a more cautious view of the upturn in the world economy since mid-2009.

In a similar vein, in October 2009, many policymakers in the US Federal Reserve Board seemed to have "expressed uncertainty about the likely strength of the upturn." So did the ECB, which suggested that the recovery "will probably be gradual." As Jörg Krämer, chief economist of Commerzbank in Frankfurt put it, the euro zone was driving ahead "with the handbrake on" (*Financial Times*, 2009aa). According to the EBRD, after a sharp contraction of a likely 6 per cent in 2009, Eastern Europe was expected to have a fragile and patchy recovery in 2010, with some economies continuing to decline in the year.

In November 2009, the OECD too expressed a cautiously optimistic view of recovery and growth. It stated that "overall, unprecedented policy efforts appear to have succeeded in limiting the severity of the downturn and fostering a recovery." However, Jorgen Elmeskov, acting head of the OECD's economics department, warned that "radical policy action will be required in the years to come to restore sound macroeconomic balance, healthy growth and low unemployment" (*Financial Times*, 2009ac). In general, economists seemed to agree that much of the recovery and rebound in global demand was due to the temporary effects of restocking by firms in industrial countries and government-sponsored stimulus spending, including an investment surge in China, and that there was still a bumpy road ahead.

In January 2010, the IMF was more optimistic as it saw a 4 per cent increase in global output for 2010 (an upward revision of three fourths of a percentage point from its estimate in October 2009), with a projected growth of 4.3 per cent in 2011 (see Table 3). In most advanced economies, the recovery was expected to be sluggish by past standards, but it would be relatively vigorous in developing and emerging economies. In the United States, output expanded at an annualized rate of 5.7 per cent in the fourth quarter of 2009 – a 6.9 per cent growth since the third quarter of 2009. Growth in emerging and developing countries was expected to rise by about 6 per cent in 2010 and it was projected to accelerate further in 2011.

The IMF also expected a stronger-than-expected rebound in capital flows. Early in 2010, the International Institute of Finance predicted that net private sector capital flows to emerging economies would jump to USD 722 billion in 2010 from USD 435 billion in 2009. Global trade, too, bounced back, as reflected in the data released by the Bureau for Economic Policy Analysis, a Dutch research institute, which showed that the volume of goods trade worldwide rose by a record rate in the fourth quarter of 2009 – 6 per cent higher than in the third quarter. Meanwhile, as already noted, big emerging economies like China and India were accelerating fast and leading recovery. On average, emerging and developing countries had less sovereign, corporate and household debt than rich countries. In line with the IMF forecast, Merrill Lynch suggested a growth rate of 6 per cent in 2010 for emerging market economies as a whole.

However, these upbeat forecasts did not come without warnings of headwinds. An unease still overshadowed the new sense of relief. The IMF called the recovery a stimulus-based "policy driven, multi-speed recovery" and expressed concerns over several potential risks, despite a significant rebound in capital flows, trade and private demand. These risks included continuing high unemployment, limited access for consumers and small enterprises to bank credit, rising government deficits and sovereign debt, and high borrowing costs for individuals and companies. Since the richest nations in the G7 carried a sovereign debt burden of USD 30 trillion, policymakers faced the difficult and politically sensitive task of balancing two seemingly conflicting demands: meeting the continuing need of ailing economies for government-backed stimulus funding, on the one hand, and scaling down the huge, and still growing, public debt, on the other. There was also the nagging problem of a gap between surplus and deficit countries, alongside a looming risk of asset-price bubbles linked to inflows of capital to emerging economies, and the need for rebalancing the world economy.

In the United States, for example, many economists attributed the increase in growth in the last two quarters of 2009 to inventory replacement. They expressed concerns that consumer spending was not sufficiently robust and that there were hardly any signs on the horizon of a job recovery robust enough to put the economy on a sustainable upward spiral. Despite the slight fall in unemployment, at least 14.8 million remained totally jobless, with more than 40 per cent unemployed for over six months. Many economists were also doubtful about the sustainability of the pace of growth and saw it more as a blip than a trend. Paul Krugman, for example, recalled as an analogy the experience of Japan, where preliminary reports in early 1996 showed that the economy was growing at an annual rate of 12 per cent, prompting claims that the country had entered a phase of self-propelled recovery. However, it turned out that Japan was only halfway through its lost decade (*The New York Times*, 2010b).

In Europe, although in February 2010, the head of the euro zone, Jean-Claude Juncker, announced a growth rate of 1 per cent for 2010, the fact that the economy grew only by 0.1 per cent in the last quarter of 2009 was raising fears of a double-dip in certain quarters.[13] A murky job outlook in Europe and the United States led Arnab Das at Roubini Global Economics in London to characterize the situation as "a recovery, but a weak, U-shaped recovery, with still an enormous slack in the market."

In China, despite an increase of 45.7 per cent in its export trade in February 2010 from a year earlier, beating forecasts, Zhu Guangyao, assistant finance minister, warned in March of an unpredictable global economic situation and suggested waiting until at least the third quarter of 2010 before deciding whether to withdraw government-provided stimulus to the economy. Also significant was a similar warning in the same month by China's commerce minister that a full recovery in exports trade might be two to three years away. Further, in a potential sign of future volatility, China's official purchasing manager's index had fallen in each of the preceding two months (*Financial Times*, 2010d). Although India was forecasting a growth rate of 8.75 per cent in the fiscal year beginning April 2010, economists were worried about a fiscal deficit of 6.8 per cent and the pressing need for infrastructure development

[13] According to the Eurostat, Germany's economy was stagnant; Italy's fell by 0.2 per cent and the French economy grew by a meagre 0.6 per cent during the last quarter of 2009.

alongside reforms in the education, health and financial sectors to sustain recovery and growth.

On the issue of rebalancing the world economy, by May 2010, there were some incipient and tentative signs that China might be willing to accept a slow rise of the renminbi while encouraging increased domestic consumption. On Saturday, 19 June 2010, just before the Toronto G20 Summit, China finally confirmed its decision to allow some flexibility in the renminbi exchange rate by pegging it to a basket of currencies (though China added that the rate would remain "basically stable"). It looked as though the US economy too was, as *The Economist* put it, "set to shift away from consumption and debt and towards export and saving." Should both these trends hold, it would help rebalancing, but a twofold constraint involving both the supply and demand sides signalled that progress was likely to be slow.

On the supply side, it was not easy for a country such as China, with an economy deeply entrenched in export promotion for both growth and job creation, to suddenly switch gears to domestically oriented production and the internal market. Moving too fast carried economic costs as well as political risks. For the United States, the switch to exports may be somewhat less difficult, but not totally cost-free, either. Three academics, namely Robert Dekle, Jonathan Eaton and Samuel Kortum, argued that even in an ideally flexible world, the switch would mean a contraction of the US economy by 0.4 per cent in real terms (Dekle et al., 2008).[14]

Also, although the current account deficit of the United States shrank from 6 per cent of GDP in 2006 to 3 per cent of GDP in 2009, the country's capacity to export critically depends on its own competitiveness and productivity growth, on the one hand, and the demand as well as the exchange rates of its trading partners, on the other hand. Few of these factors, especially the demand from the rest of the rich world afflicted by the economic downturn, are likely to change significantly any time soon.

On the demand side, private consumption in China has long been low, accounting for only 37 per cent of GDP, compared with 71 per cent of GDP for the United States prior to the crisis, according to McKinsey Global Institute. Although more recently, Chinese consumption has been rising rather fast, inadequate social safety nets, combined with past experience of periods of economic hardship and deep-seated cultural traits strengthening the propensity to save, would set limits to consumption.

[14] Authors' note: At the extreme, US GDP falls by 30 per cent relative to world GDP. Because of the pervasiveness of non-traded goods, however, most domestic prices move in parallel with relative GDP, so that changes in real GDP are small.

As for the United States, it is true that anti-thrift institutions and policies were in retreat; that instead of pushing credit cards, companies like American Express were encouraging customers to use their debit (charge) cards; and that the consumer binge had clearly ended (*The Economist*, 2010a). Not surprisingly, the US-based Pew Research Center found that personal savings that had dropped to 2 per cent in 2007 went up to 4 per cent in 2009. Even so, the immediate need to use stimulus spending in order to boost consumer demand through job creation and wage growth precluded the possibility of raising any time soon the level of savings to, say, 9 per cent, as had been the average between 1950 and 1980. In fact, a model developed by the US President's Council of Economic Advisers predicted that it would eventually settle at between 4 per cent and 7 per cent (*The Economist*, 2010a).

To sum up, although economic growth had turned positive since the third quarter of 2009, global recovery was expected to be sluggish in a still fragile and unbalanced world economy, with demand dampened, credit still limited for consumers, and small and medium industries and joblessness continuing to persist (for information on more recent economic outlook, see Annexes I and II). Several of these negative elements were closely interlinked, with strong feedback between them, as briefly explained below.

Why job recovery is so important

If credit was constrained and banks were not lending enough either to businesses or consumers, as was the case in the United States and in the euro zone, what were the reasons behind it? Many banks were still just limping along, despite generous government bailouts.

However, even the banks that had the financial wherewithal, such as Goldman Sachs and JP Morgan in the United States, which made combined profits of USD 7 billion in the third quarter of 2009, were making money more from trading complex financial products than through lending.[15] Similarly, in the euro zone, bank lending to businesses remained negative between February and August in 2009, and loans to households showed little growth over 2008, despite ECB president Jean-Claude Trichet's appeal to banks to provide credit to oil the wheels of recovery.

If constraints imposed by banks were contributing to the slowdown in bank lending, a more basic problem was falling consumer confidence and consumer demand. Even if banks were willing and had the necessary wherewithal, they

[15] Business financing fell to USD 1.411 trillion in 2009, down USD 179 billion from a year earlier (2008). Consumer lending by commercial banks stood at USD 834 billion in August 2009, down USD 45 billion from figures at the end of 2008.

cannot lend unless there is effective business and consumer demand. However, businesses are not likely to borrow and invest unless they can be reasonably sure of effective consumer demand. Also, in the absence of a significant improvement in jobs and earnings, consumers would be hamstrung either to spend to raise the level of demand or to save in order to deleverage their debt. Boosting consumer demand on a stable and sustainable basis requires programmes for direct job creation; temporary incentives such as rebates for home buying and cash for clunkers are not enough and may even have some perverse effects. Some economists, Jeffrey Sachs, for example, likened such temporary incentives to "offering one more drink on the government account to overcome mass hangover."

As mentioned earlier, part of the growth in 2009 was also due to an adjustment in inventory levels (restocking of shelves helped to boost output), but the effect was expected to fade soon. Further, if the increase in consumer spending is at the cost of the personal saving rate – as was the case in the United States, where the rate fell to 3.4 per cent in the third quarter of 2009 from 4.9 per cent in the second quarter – then it will not help ease the household debt problem. This shows the critical importance of job recovery (further discussed in the next section).

Some analysts were setting store by the more recent upsurge in export trade, especially in Asia, as an engine for recovery. However, export-led recovery cannot last long if private demand, both business and consumer, in the rest of the world economy falters; this would restrain the growth of the export-oriented countries themselves. As the IMF put it: "If signs of renewed external environment weakness were to rise, the positive feedback loop triggered in Asia could shift into reverse." In fact, as noted earlier, the EU was already worried that the huge expansion of China's industrial capacity, fed by massive stimulus spending, could threaten a surge of cheap exports and lead to a protectionist backlash (*Financial Times*, 2009af).

A the same time, a sudden outburst of just business demand, fuelled by an influx of at least partly speculative foreign capital, as was happening most recently in Latin America and Asia, could raise the spectre of future asset bubbles.[16] This needs to be managed (without prejudice to sound consumer demand) by adopting counterbalancing fiscal and monetary policies, especially to discourage speculation. In Asia, there was a potential danger of asset bubbles as the economic upswing and excessive monetary liquidity portended to be accompanied by rising equity and housing prices. If not tamed in time, this could "threaten again to destroy livelihoods and trap

[16] In 2009, reversing erstwhile trends, emerging markets as a whole saw a record USD 89 billion inflow of foreign capital.

millions of people in poverty" (*Financial Times*, 2009ae). By the beginning of 2010, China had started putting some brakes on bank loans and excessive monetary liquidity to avert the danger. Meanwhile, Brazil had already introduced a 2 per cent tax on capital inflows to equity and bond markets; Colombia's central bank announced it would buy dollars to stem the rise of the peso; and Peru was pondering limits on the foreign exchange exposure of its banks. India, on the other hand, was raising interest rates.

For the reasons discussed in the next section, a prolonged stagnation in the labour markets of rich countries, in terms of jobs and wages, seemed most likely. This portended a slow pace of economic recovery, and slow recovery does not help job growth, thereby creating a stubborn vicious circle.

Time lag between output recovery and employment recovery: How would it affect labour markets and migration?

Past experience shows that labour market recovery lags behind economic recovery by four to five years (see Figure 2). A paper by Reinhart and Rogoff (2008), spanning experiences of financial crises over centuries, seemed to suggest that the joblessness caused by a typical financial crisis could continue for four to five years.

Figure 2: Output recovery versus job recovery

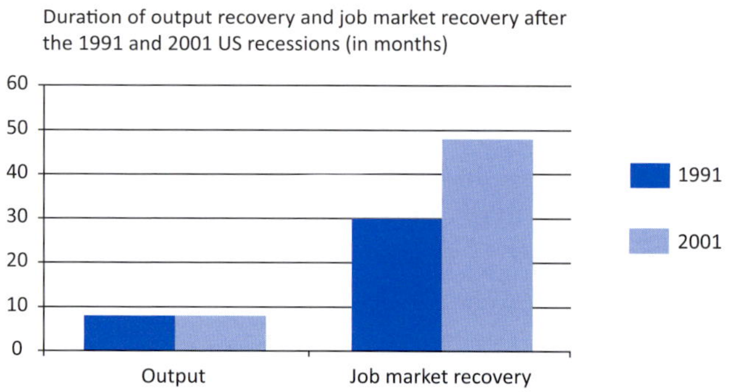

Source: Irons, 2009.

Also, as the US experience shows, the time for job market recovery to materialize seems to have increased in recent years, with the pace of job growth slowing down with each economic recovery. Both the 1991 and 2001 recessions lasted eight months, but the job market recovery took 30 months for the 1991 recession and 48 months for the 2001 recession (Irons, 2009).[17] Before 1990, it took an average of 21 months to regain the jobs shed during a recession. Also, significantly, in the last two recoveries since the 1980s, it took substantially more economic growth to achieve comparable increases in employment than in the previous ones. Europe, too, has had similar experiences. As Ronald Janssen of the European Trades Union Confederation put it: "In the last decade, it was thought you needed around 1.5 per cent [growth to stabilize employment]; in the [present] recovery, the figure could be closer to 2.5 or 3 per cent" (*Financial Times*, 2010i).

In analysing the most recent trends in the US labour market, most experts believed that this time, significant new hiring would take many more months, if not years, to emerge (see Figure 3). Heidi Shierholz of the Washington, D.C.-based Economic Policy Institute, for example, forecast that (US) unemployment would remain "elevated for four years to come" (*The New York Times*, 2009e).

Figure 3: A jobless recovery in the United States

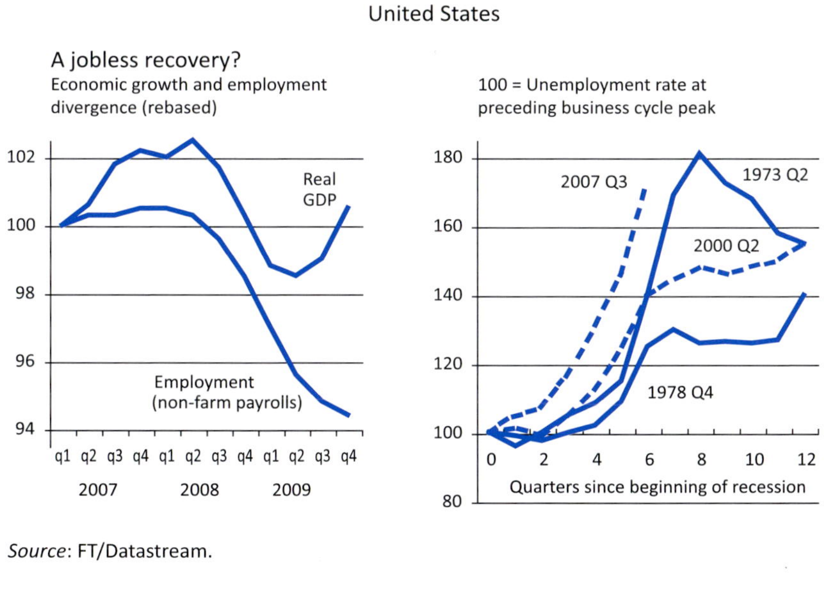

Source: FT/Datastream.

[17] Some have estimated that the time lag during the two previous recessions was 31 months and 46 months, respectively. According to some experts, the basic functioning of the US economy itself changed in ways that slowed down the pace of job growth even during economic expansion. The number of private sector jobs increased about 3.5 per cent a year during periods of economic expansion in the 1950s, 1960s and 1970s. During expansion in the 1980s and 1990s, jobs grew 2.4 per cent annually; and during the last decade, job growth was just 0.9 per cent a year.

On 3 June 2009, Ben Bernanke, chairman of the Federal Reserve, said that job recovery in the United States might take two to three years. This was echoed in November by Janet Yellen, president of the Federal Reserve Bank of San Francisco, who thought unemployment "could well stay high for several years to come" (*Financial Times*, 2009x). A similar view was taken by Richard Trumka, president of the AFL-CIO, the country's largest labour union, who thought that (in the absence of new large-scale construction projects) real job creation could be delayed until 2012. Most analysts seemed to agree that, in the absence of job growth, consumer demand would be a laggard, and constitute a defining feature of slow recovery (*The New York Times*, 2009i).

For the OECD countries as a whole, by the fourth quarter of 2009, the unemployment rate was hovering at around 8.8 per cent, which implied 18 million unemployed persons. This seemed to suggest a slight improvement over the OECD's earlier unemployment rate projection of 10 per cent at the end of 2010, but the future situation still looked uncertain.

For the United States, in January 2010, a bit of cheerful news came with the US Department of Labor announcing that the unemployment rate had fallen to 9.7 per cent from 10 per cent in December 2009. However, there were no escaping concerns about the job market, as the Department also reported a loss of 20,000 jobs in January and revised upwards the overall toll of the recession on the job market since December 2007 at 8.4 million, nearly 1 million more than previously reported. The number of people filing first-time unemployment benefit claims also rose by 8,000 to 480,000 in January. In the same month, the Congressional Budget Office recognized the stark reality of the situation, announcing that unemployment would stay at 10 per cent in the first half of 2010 and would probably not return to the more normal level of 5 per cent for another six years or so.

In a similar vein, the US President's annual *Economic Report to Congress*, issued in February 2010, expected the US economy to create an average of 95,000 jobs per month, and admitted that this would not be enough to make a dent in the huge backlog of unemployment. However, the report foresaw an improvement in the employment situation in 2011, with the creation of a monthly average of 190,000 jobs, and even better progress in 2012.

Many independent economists were also doubtful that the erstwhile improvement in employment indicated the start of a positive trend. Although the average workweek rose slightly from 33.8 per cent to 33.9 per cent in January 2010, businesses were reluctant to add full-time positions. As the owner of a small business put it: "I am very frugal with my decisions. For us to hire, we need to see a turn in the economy" (*The New York Times*, 2010d).

Some forecasts were still suggesting that the jobless rate would reach nearly 11 per cent by the end of 2010.

The picture seemed to have changed a little for the better in March 2010, as the US Department of Labor announced the addition of 162,000 non-farm jobs. However, analysts pointed out that the March 2010 figure may have been inflated by a rebound in February, when many people could not work due to snowstorms. Also, nearly a third of the new recruitment was for temporary work on the 2010 census. The economy still needed to add more than 100,000 jobs a month to absorb new entrants to the labour force, besides providing employment for the nearly 15 million Americans already looking for work. Meanwhile, the increase in temporary workers – many employers were still testing the waters – increased the broader measure of unemployment and underemployment to 16.9 per cent from 16.8 per cent in February 2010. Also, the average length of time the jobless had been out of work reached 31.2 weeks, the longest period since 1948. Significantly, in declaring the March job recovery as a "beginning to turn the corner," US President Obama was careful to add that "it will take time to achieve the strong and sustained job growth that we need." Indeed, in May 2010, the US economy added just 41,000 private sector jobs, falling well short of market expectations. The headline increase of 431,000 in non-farm payrolls was swollen by the temporary hiring of 411,000 workers in the public sector to complete the national census. The unemployment rate fell from 9.9 per cent to 9.7 per cent, but the drop was helped by discouraged job hunters pulling out of the labour market.

Several reasons explain why job recovery generally lags behind output recovery and why this is likely to be so in the present economic crisis:

First, most employers resume normal staff recruitment once they are convinced that the post-recession recovery will be sustainable. For the most recent recession, as of September 2009, this was not yet the case in the majority of rich countries. Many employers were afraid that once massive aid under various government stimulus plans and monetary easing were withdrawn, economies could slide back into recession. As discussed earlier, most employers, like economists, were considering the incipient recovery to be too fragile to justify restarting normal staff recruitment. Fearful of a double-dip or W-shaped recovery, some were being even more cautious.

Second, in a number of countries, public sector schemes – such as the short-shift scheme in Germany and the *chomage partiel* in France – were helping private employers, often complementing employers' own programmes, to either retain part of the staff that would otherwise be retrenched or work out temporary layoff arrangements. More than 20 countries, mainly European ones, introduced or expanded short-time work schemes during the recent recession. Unutilized staff resources thus gave companies the option to deal with incremental output growth without adding new full-time staff to their payroll.

The continuing slack in the labour market also made it easy for employers to recruit temporary and part-time workers on short notice, when necessary. In Germany, for example, many industry groups sought production and staff flexibility by hiring more temporary workers and using external service companies. In France, hours billed by temporary staffing agencies rose by 4 per cent in February and by 12 per cent in March 2010. In Germany, hours worked rose 24 per cent, whereas in Italy, hours worked increased by 20 per cent in March.

The situation largely explains why, despite recent output growth alongside significant staff reductions, the wages of existing company personnel were not rising or rising much more slowly than in the pre-recession years. In the United States, for example, although average monthly wages were 3.1 per cent higher in May 2009 compared to May 2008, month-to-month increases in April and May 2009 were only 0.1 per cent, and wages for manufacturing workers fell 0.1 per cent, according to the US Department of Labor. Even in case of a rise in hourly rates, average weekly earnings were adversely affected as employers slashed working hours; in September 2008, working hours were cut by a tenth of an hour to 33 hours (US Department of Labor, 2009). As will be further discussed in chapter 4, wages and benefits rose by a meagre 1.5 per cent in 2009. In another sign of long-term pressure on middle-class wages, median family income, an important source of consumer demand, fell to USD 50,300 in 2008, compared with USD 52,200 the year before, wiping out the income gains of the previous three years. The 2008 figure, adjusted for inflation, was lower than the median family income a decade earlier.

In the UK, research by the Bank of England shows that real wages have risen by just 0.1 per cent in the current crisis, compared with a 7.3 per cent rise in the 1990s. Wage stagnation also largely explains why during the 2008–2009 recession, employment fell by just 1.9 per cent (adding to existing unemployment), although the economy contracted by 6.2 per cent. This was in comparison with a 3.4 per cent drop in employment in the early 1990s recession, when output fell only by 2.5 per cent. Retention of workers was largely responsible for the relatively small decline in both wages and employment. The Bank of England warned that this was one reason why there were still great risks of further increase in unemployment in the UK should production and demand not return as quickly as companies expected (Bank of England, 2010).

As in the past, this might imply that even as economic growth resumes, workers may lag behind in terms of jobs, wage growth, and wealth or sustainable upward mobility. This in turn would constrain consumer demand. Since consumption is one of the main drivers of a faltering economy, consumer demand would slow down the pace of economic recovery itself, creating a vicious circle.

The situation becomes even more vicious and worrisome for another reason. As already noted, experiences of previous jobless recovery in both the United States and Europe since the 1980s showed that it would take substantially more economic growth to achieve comparable increases in employment than in previous recovery phases. However, such robust economic growth will remain elusive unless job market and consumer demand start to bounce back. As the 31 January 2010 editorial of *The New York Times* crisply put it, "no jobs, no recovery." Breaking the vicious circle in a most judicious way and ensuring that growth in output and jobs reinforce each other would be one of the most challenging tasks for policymakers (this is further discussed in chapter 4).

The impact of the present economic crisis on world labour markets, more specifically on employment and earnings, as well as on poverty and inequality, as broadly outlined above, will continue to be a major factor in shaping labour or economically motivated migration at both ends of the flow. It will also have an effect, if somewhat indirectly, on certain other types of movement such as family reunification and humanitarian flows. The analysis in the next chapter reflects this perspective.

2. The crisis and its impact on the pattern of migration: Changing trends in flows and stocks

The economic and social ramifications of the present crisis, especially its ravages on job markets, are sure to have a significant impact on the future configuration of international migration. However, at the time of writing, continuing uncertainty about the shape of future recovery makes it difficult to foresee clearly the effects of the crisis on migration, especially from a long-term perspective. The difficulty also stems from the relative paucity of detailed information about what actually happened to migration during past economic crises, including the Great Depression. The fact that, as already discussed, the contextual circumstances governing past crises vary widely only adds to the difficulty.

And yet it is possible, and indeed important, to discern some of the recent policy trends and practices triggered by the recession and their likely effects on the configuration of migration. This is important especially because analysis would help avoid some of the possible knee-jerk, and often self-defeating, reactions in the form of, for example, panicky dismissal of immigrant workers by employers and draconian restrictions imposed by policymakers on new immigration. It can also be helpful in sharpening both government and public vigilance against possible abuse of the human and labour rights of migrants or the rise of anti-immigrant feeling that could lead to social conflicts and xenophobia and retard global recovery.

The present crisis, like its predecessors, will surely not last forever. It is important to remember, though, that some of the policy or practical measures taken during a crisis could have long-term effects on the future configuration of migration. It took several decades for international migration to recover from the impact of restrictive immigration measures that countries such as the United States[18] and France took just before and during the Great Depression and the social climate created by these actions. Numbers aside, changes in the age composition and labour market characteristics of new migrants could have an enduring effect. Equally important, if migration is not effectively managed during a crisis and it becomes a source of serious tension and conflict, host countries could be unduly reluctant to admit immigrants for many years to come. All of these considerations guide the discussion that follows in this chapter.

[18] The US Immigration Act of 1924, which went into effect in 1928, imposed serious quota restrictions on the annual flow of new immigrants from most countries.

2.1 New immigration

Alongside falling labour demand and dwindling opportunities for legal entry, a restrictive immigration climate is developing in many destination countries

As the 2008–2009 crisis led to a fall in the overall demand for labour and the future looked uncertain, a restrictive immigration climate gained ground in almost all destination countries, both developed and developing, and opportunities for legal entry continued to dwindle, especially for labour migrants.

Governments can regulate labour migration in three main ways: by fixing numerical limits or quotas, by establishing labour shortage lists, and by conducting labour market tests, including the requirement of a job offer prior to entry. Many governments used these various instruments to reduce labour migration in response to the crisis (OECD, 2010a). The examples cited below are indicative of this trend:

In the United States, the admission of migrants, including skilled migrants, holding temporary work visas slowed significantly. The Troubled Assets Recovery Program (TARP) 2009 banned aid-receiving companies from applying for H-1B visas for highly skilled foreign workers if they had recently laid off American workers. Although the caps for temporary migrants under H-1A and H-1B visas have not changed over the past few years and have always been oversubscribed, there was pressure to further lower these caps. In 2009, Senator Chuck Grassley of Iowa, for example, urged curbs on the number of H-1B visas, in view of the deteriorating unemployment situation. The recession had no doubt reduced the demand from companies for H-1B visas, but by December 2009 the cap had been reached, with more than enough applications received over eight months to allot the 65,000 visas available for fiscal year 2010. However, according to official sources, over 25,000 business companies participating in the programme were to be audited for verification of the validity of their requests – more than five times the number of audits conducted in 2009. In other words, aside from the TARP-related restrictions, enforcement of existing caps was tightened.

There were several other indications of a decline in new labour immigration flows in the United States. Under the US system, employers must apply for certification of their job offer; that is, they must show that the offer meets standards in terms of prevailing wages and other conditions for a comparable job. Once the certification is received, employers may apply for the relevant visas. In effect, between 2007 and 2009, there was a significant fall in certification applications for permanent employment visas, as well as in the number of certifications actually issued under the H-1B programme for skilled workers and the H-2B programme for short-term workers. As in 2009 for H-1B visas, the actual visa requests for both types of temporary workers were slow to come by in 2010.

There was, however, at least one narrow immigration stream in the United States that gained new life as a consequence of the recession. This was the US immigrant investor (EB-5) visa programme, which grants lawful permanent residence to foreigners who invest USD 500,000 or USD 1 million, depending on whether the money is invested in targeted employment areas (where unemployment is at least 150% of the national average) or in any US business and creates or preserves at least 10 US jobs. The number of approved EB-5 visas nearly tripled between fiscal years 2008 and 2009 from 1,443 to 4,218, according to the US State Department. Nearly 90 per cent of EB-5 investors were estimated to have invested in rural or targeted employment areas.

Policymakers, including Senators Patrick Leahy and Jeff Sessions, were therefore active in promoting the programme as a tool to create jobs in recession-hit local economies (Chishti and Bergeron, 2009). The programme, however, was still a temporary one, and despite the increase in its popularity, the number of visas issued in 2009 was still less than half of the annual allocation, and carried only limited potential impact.

Canada established a shortlist for applications to its skilled employment entry channel, and made it a requirement for those without sponsorship to have an occupation on the shortage list to be eligible. After peaking in the second quarter of 2008, authorization of temporary foreign workers fell by 57 per cent through the third quarter of 2009.

In Europe, a number of countries that had previously witnessed large inflows of migrants, especially labour migrants, experienced a significant decline in inflows. These countries include Spain, Ireland, Italy and the UK. Spain sharply reduced its annual regional ceilings for non-seasonal labour migrants to a total of 901 for 2009 and to less than 200 for 2010, compared to 15,700 in 2008. Under the general regime (which exempts nominal requests from a labour market test), the country's intake of labour migrants fell from more than 20,000 in 2007 to 16,000 in 2009, with less than 2,000 entries in the first quarter of 2010. As the crisis led to fewer opportunities in other sectors, more Spaniards and resident foreigners returned to agriculture and took on farming jobs. The result was that the seasonal worker programme saw a sharper fall of new inflows, from 65,000 in 2007 to only 3,600 in 2009.

Foreseeing lower labour demand, Italy, which had set a maximum cap of 170,000 in 2007 for non-EU workers, lowered its ceiling for 2008 to 150,000, confining it mainly to domestic and personal care work and accepting migrants from the backlog of applications made in 2007. It also decided to set a quota of zero for non-seasonal work in 2009. In both Finland and the Netherlands, the number of applications for work permits fell. In Finland, the monthly number, which had peaked in mid-2008, had since fallen below half that level; in the Netherlands, the number was down 38 per cent in 2009 compared with 2006. In France, the number of temporary workers fell from 9,200 in 2008 to 4,800 in 2009. In Iceland, one of the hardest-hit OECD countries, labour immigration in the second half of 2008 fell to a third of the level during the previous year and dropped to almost zero in early 2009 (OECD, 2009).

In November 2008, the UK decided to cut back its originally planned target of 1 million skilled migrants to 800,000 to meet special shortages in specific occupations. A year later, in November 2009, the government confirmed that it would accept an advisory committee's recommendation to remove civil and aircraft engineers, hospital consultants and ships officers from the skill shortages list. This implied that the number of jobs open to non-EU workers would dip from 530,000 to 500,000 (*Financial Times*, 2009z). The number of visas issued under the UK's employer-requested and labour market-tested (Tier 2) programme was more than 35 per cent lower in 2009 than in 2008.

The UK government suspended recruitment of non-EU workers for low-skilled occupations and made changes to the points-based system for admission of foreign workers. It tightened labour market tests for certain skilled jobs and raised the standards for admission of foreign workers for some other types of jobs (UK Border Agency, 2009). Explaining the objectives of the change, the Home Secretary stated: "It is right in a downturn to be more selective about the skill levels of those migrants and to do more for British workers first" (UK Border Agency, 2009). The tougher entry requirements were estimated to decrease the number of non-EU skilled workers by half (Ford, 2009). At the same time, applications from nationals of the eight newly admitted EU states (so-called A8 countries, which joined the EU in 2004), including in particular those from Poland, dropped from 53,000 in the last quarter of 2007 to 29,000 over the same period in 2008. In 2010, the new Conservative Party-led government announced a temporary general cap of 241,000 on new non-EU entries, despite resistance from the Liberal Democratic Party, its junior coalition partner.

Sharp reductions were made in the shortage lists of most countries where the list provided an exemption from labour market tests. Within the OECD, the countries that did so included Australia, Canada, Ireland, New Zealand, Spain and the UK.

Australia cut more than half the occupations on its shortage list, barring entry for bricklaying, plumbing, carpentry and electrical jobs – occupations that had seen a drop-off in demand. Monthly applications for temporary skilled migrant workers fell by 62 per cent, compared with peak levels reached in June 2008. Australia, like New Zealand, however, remained committed to attracting foreign students as potential skilled migrants. New Zealand left its target for permanent economic migrants unchanged and kept open the channel for temporary migrants for certain economic branches or occupations, but it scaled back its immediate shortage list by nearly a third in mid-2009. Between the first quarter of 2009 and 2010, quarterly applications for temporary workers fell 46 per cent.

The UK, like the United States, tightened applications for entry programmes based on labour market tests. Canada introduced a stricter review of requests for low-skilled temporary workers. A number of countries saw the rate of rejection of applications for work permits rise due to the downturn; for instance, the rate of application rejection in Finland increased from 10 per cent to 27 per cent even as the number of requests fell, while in Ireland the figure rose from 11 per cent in 2007 to 22 per cent in 2009.

The combined effect of falling labour demand and more restrictive or stringent application of entry programmes resulted in fewer actual labour migration entries in most OECD countries. The traditional settlement countries in the OECD set targets for permanent employment migration. These too were slightly reduced due to the crisis. Australia, for example, lowered the quota for permanent skilled migrants from 133,000 to 108,100 for 2009 and 113,850 for 2010. Canada lowered its target for permanent economic migrants by about 2 per cent for the financial year 2008–2009, but raised it by 8.3 per cent for 2010. In the United States, data from the Department of Homeland Security suggested a slowdown in admission of certain types of permanent immigrants in 2009. Overall, the inflow of immigrants to OECD countries fell by about 6 per cent to 4.4 million persons in 2008, reversing an average annual increase of 11 per cent over five years. National data suggested a further fall in immigration to OECD countries in 2009 (OECD, 2009).

In Eastern Europe, the Russian Federation reduced its quota of new immigrants from 4 million to 2 million, and Kazakhstan decided to put a moratorium on the entry of unskilled or less-skilled workers. The Czech Republic and Poland opted for a stricter review of requests for entry of temporary workers and, like Lithuania, reduced their shortage lists. Bulgaria extended the time that a job offer under labour market tests must be publicized locally.

In Asia, Malaysia revoked the job visas of 55,000 Bangladeshi immigrants and Thailand decided not to renew work permits for half a million migrant workers or issue new work permits. On 21 January 2009, Malaysia sharply reduced new recruitment of migrant workers, banning new entries of foreigners to fill jobs in manufacturing and services in order to make jobs available for nationals. From January to February 2007, the authorities approved 800 employer requests for new migrant workers each day; in the same period in 2008, the number fell to 250 a day (Migration News, 2009b). Like Malaysia, Thailand encouraged employers to lay off migrant workers in order to make room for domestic workers. The Republic of Korea reduced the quota of foreign workers from 100,000 in 2008 to 34,000 in 2009, and then to 24,000 in 2010; it also doubled the length of time that a job offer must be publicized locally. In addition, the Republic of Korea fixed, for the first time, a quota of 17,000 for ethnic Koreans who previously did not need employment visas under the quota system, and put a halt to this category of entrance in 2010.

In Latin America, data released by the Mexican government showed that for the year ended August 2008, emigration declined by 226,000 persons or 25 per cent, compared with the previous year. Net outflows (i.e. those who left minus those who returned) fell by half during the same period, according to the National Institute of Statistics and Geography (*The New York Times*, 2009c).

What is the overall impact of these and other restrictions on new flows of labour migration? Much of course depends on the duration of the crisis and the shape of recovery. Historical evidence in the United States does not indicate a long-term correlation between legal immigration flows and normal business cycles. However, the present economic crisis is not a "normal" business cycle downturn: not only is it truly global, it is also much deeper. Furthermore, it has been running for a longer period than most normal business cycles, and, at the time of writing, the outlook remains uncertain.

More importantly, as already discussed, any improvement in the labour market in terms of jobs and earnings is sure to lag behind output recovery for quite some time. It is likely, though not certain, that output recovery will help avoid panicky reactions on the part of both employers and policymakers in destination countries to curb new migration inflows, but depressed labour market conditions will certainly act as a drag on labour demand and stand in the way of early reversal of the current slowdown in migration. There are several additional reasons for this:

First, the depth of the downturn, especially in the manufacturing sector (despite some tentative positive signs), clearly implies that full recovery will involve considerable economic restructuring; that is, declining industries and obsolete technologies will be replaced by new industries and more efficient technologies. This in turn will invariably demand new skills and aptitudes. Some of the laid-off migrant workers, including those who may have already stopped looking for jobs and left the country, will be unable to respond to this shift in labour market needs and reverse the erstwhile slowdown in migration.

Second, should there be large-scale unemployment among migrants in host countries and considerable delay in job-market recovery, there could be a real risk that the channels for labour market information, including social network links, would be weakened, constraining new flows.

Third, as noted earlier, if migration is badly managed during a crisis, leading to social unrest and conflicts, the host country is likely to be more responsive to populist anti-immigrant slogans and campaigns. If this feeling takes hold and becomes widely entrenched, policymakers may be unable or unwilling to admit as many migrants as they have admitted in the past. This could thus have an inhibiting effect on migration for a long time to come.

There is yet another consideration. Labour migration is largely influenced by the intercountry wage and employment differential and comparative future prospects. Conditions in the source country matter. If, owing to higher rates of economic growth, origin countries achieve faster recovery than destination countries and this trend is anticipated to continue, people in source countries may be less inclined to move to the same destination countries. An econometric study in the UK argued that a potentially higher rate of growth and employment in countries that send migrants to the UK would lead to a fall in net immigration to the latter – 50,000 less by 2015 – than in a non-recession scenario (UK Department for Communities and Local Government, 2009).

Economic forecasts suggest that countries such as China, India and Brazil will continue to have positive economic growth, though perhaps at lower rates than those in the recent past, and that recovery will be faster in these countries than in many traditional destination countries. Narrowing the intercountry wage and employment differential and the anticipated future prospects of the home-country economy may induce some types of workers, for example, skilled persons in specific sectors, to stay at home rather than move. The situation in Poland foreshadowed similar trends.

At the global level, however, this would reduce total new migration flows only if the growth and employment differential narrows between sending and origin countries collectively as groups. Otherwise, migration flows could just be diverted to new destination countries with more promising earnings and job prospects. This could, among other things, lead to increased intraregional migration in some regions such as Asia.

Finally, if the recovery continues to be sluggish for several years or if the process is reversed, policymakers may be inclined to take active measures to reduce labour migration in response to an increasing labour reserve and perceived future labour market trends, or due to the pressure of public opinion.

The short-term impact of the crisis on lowering new labour immigration flows may be attenuated by some mitigating factors. For instance, in the past, job-related visas in countries such as the United States were often oversubscribed and visas were issued in a chronological order using the backlog of applications. As noted earlier, although there was a slowdown in demand for H-1B visas due to the recession, the annual cap on 65,000 visas available for fiscal year 2010 was reached in December 2009. Even if there were a fall in the number of applications, this was not likely to affect new employment-based immigration in the short term because of the backlog of applications. However, where labour-market tests are employed, requiring employers to prove that they made an effort to recruit locally, temporary new flows may suffer, as unemployment may lead workers already in the country to move to sectors where jobs are available. Experience shows, however, the limitations of such an adjustment – this may be due to a skills mismatch, as already discussed, or to geographic distance and dislocation and other constraints inhibiting labour mobility.

There is also the question of time needed for processing visa applications for labour immigration, which varies widely between countries and between categories. In the United States, for example, the time lag for employment-based permanent migration could be four to eight years, and the jobs may disappear during the waiting period. Many OECD countries require confirmation that the job in question still exists after the issuance of a visa and the entry of the foreigner. The Republic of Korea goes even further by requiring the signing of a valid contract before a visa is granted. In such cases, long delays in visa processing and rapid changes in the labour market could create a real problem in ensuring smooth new flows. When, as in the case of the United States, employment-based visas open the way to permanent migration, the delay would imply no change in the stock of employment-based visa holders, which, in the current restrictive immigration climate, can be used as an argument to lower the target of new admission for this category.

Labour migration, however, is only one component of total migration flows. A number of countries both within and outside the OECD accept flows of immigration that are much less sensitive to changes in labour market or economic conditions. These include family reunification, refugee flows and other humanitarian intakes. These migration flows are sometimes called "non-discretionary" in the sense that governments have less direct administrative control in regulating them. The effects of the recession on total migration would clearly be more limited in countries where these flows account for a large share of total flows.

Overall, the effects of the recession, whether short-term or long-term, on new migration cannot be isolated from policy measures to manage migration and public attitudes to it. Governments have more flexibility in attuning the level of temporary labour migration to trends in the job market. However, this flexibility to manoeuvre could be perilous in the event of a faulty decision made out of panic or as a result of populist pressure, for example, excessive cuts in annual quotas of temporary migrants or unduly restrictive labour market tests.

Even in the case of so-called non-discretionary flows, such pressure may induce policymakers to lower immigration, for example, by setting or reducing quotas and changing the eligibility criteria for family reunification or refugee flows. A number of OECD countries did impose more restrictions on family reunification by tightening the criteria for admission. Spain and Italy both limited reunification for some parents, and the minimum age for spousal reunification was increased in several countries such as Denmark, Italy and the UK. France and the Netherlands introduced language and other tests for some categories of family reunification (OECD, 2010a).

It is worth noting that public vigilance, notably the proactive stance of civil society against such restrictions, may constrain inroads into acquired rights or denigrate bilateral and international commitments. In the EU, for example, a directive sets some limits on the power of member states to curtail family reunification (OECD, 2010a: 43).

As indicated at the beginning of the section, policy trends and practices in most receiving countries are geared towards lowering new migration, especially labour migration. If anti-immigration feeling gains further ground among the public, governments may feel impelled to take precipitous action to make such measures even more stringent. There were some ominous indications that such anti-immigrant feeling is on the rise and the danger it poses cannot be ignored. An April 2009 Harris/*Financial Times* poll, for example, revealed that the majority of the population in the UK and Germany opposed citizens of other EU countries getting jobs in their countries. Equally, if not more, revealing was the result of a survey carried out by the Pew Research Center in the fall of 2009 that showed that the majority of the population in five EU countries – namely Italy, Spain, the UK, Germany and France – were in favour of further restrictions on immigration; the percentage was above 75 per cent for the first three of these countries (see Figure 4).

Figure 4: Public attitudes towards immigration restrictions and controls (%)

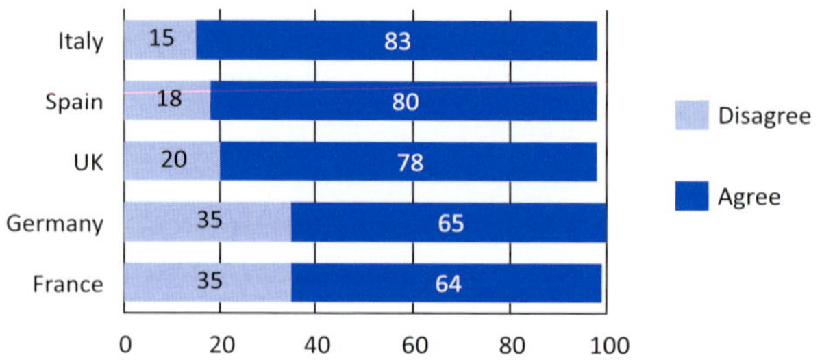

Source: Pew Research Center, 2009a.

What then is the conclusion? A slowdown in new labour migration flows, especially of less-skilled migrants and temporary migrants, is already evident and is likely to continue in the short run. The slowdown will be largely demand-driven, but policy measures such as fixing entry ceilings below the level of effective demand (as in Italy and the Republic of Korea, for example), as well as the stringent application of entry programmes and increased rejection of employers' applications, will continue to play a part. As for the medium- to long-term effects, these will depend largely on the duration of the crisis and the shape of recovery in sending and source countries and also on how migration is managed during the crisis. Ongoing restrictive measures are most likely to have at least a mild restraining effect on new migration in the medium term, alongside a shift in the composition of migration flows.

In OECD countries, the change in the composition of total migration will be of some particular significance. In most OECD countries, new immigrants will be mostly too young or too old to be in the labour force, and those who are of working age will come from family reunification and humanitarian streams with traditionally low employment rates. As a paper by OECD (2010a) put it, the mix of these factors "makes it likely that employment outcomes for immigrants in the near term will worsen before they improve." This points to a constraint as well as a challenge for labour market integration policies for immigrants in the recovery phase (further discussed in chapter 4).

These and other contextual developments, such as high youth unemployment in a number of OECD countries, may have an attenuating effect even on the underlying factors that drive migration over time, including labour market asymmetry between countries and pent-up demand for skills, demographic imbalances and growing concerns related to social security funding among rich countries.[19] Also, as already argued, if out of panic or extreme populist

[19] However, as discussed in chapter 5, the situation could change over the longer term due to a possible decline in both the pull and push factors driving migration.

pressure, governments take draconian action and further harden ongoing restrictions, this could create some longer-term, built-in constraints on new migration flows. Government policies and practices on migration and public attitudes to it during and in the immediate aftermath of a crisis therefore remain important from a long-term perspective as well.

2.2 Return migration

Can migrants be coaxed and cajoled to return?

Just as economic crises tend to lower new migration, especially demand-driven labour flows, they also encourage return migration. Here again it is not just the conditions in the receiving countries but also those in the source countries that matter. In times of lack of opportunities and possible hardships in receiving countries, migrants may be inclined to return to their homelands, especially if they still have some family and social ties and can harness some support. However, if economic woes are much worse and the future looks even grimmer in their home country, migrants may decide to stay on in the host country or, if possible, move to a third country. As noted, during the Great Depression in the 1930s, some 500,000 European migrants returned to southern Europe from the United States, and the number of Mexicans in the United States fell by some 40 per cent.

In times of falling labour demand, the host country may find it politically expedient to encourage migrants to return home and may decide to offer some incentives so that the jobs occupied by migrants can be freed for local workers. In the wake of the oil crisis and the ban on labour immigration in 1973–1974, most labour-importing Western European countries offered incentive packages to encourage migrants to return home. As for irregular migrants, the receiving country may decide simply to expel them, as Malaysia and Thailand tried to do during the 1997–1998 Asian financial crisis.

The present crisis has led to some similar developments. A survey in Ireland late in 2008 indicated that one third of 200,000 Polish migrant workers expected to return within a year. Over 600,000 Filipino migrants, mostly women working in electronics factories in Taiwan Province of China and men working in construction industries in the Middle East, returned home before the end of their contracts in the first quarter of 2009. Although the economic downturn in the host country and rising unemployment were the main drivers of return in most cases, the specific circumstances often varied from country to country.

For Polish migrants in countries such as the UK, these circumstances included the relative strength of the Polish economy, which was showing some resilience to the downturn, and better prospects of return to the host country once recovery begins, given the short distance to Poland and low travel costs. The fact that many Polish migrants had in any case intended to return home after limited periods of time in the host country also played a part.

Poland, however, has not seen a massive return of its migrants. In 2007, fearing a global economic downturn, Donald Tusk, Poland's prime minister, set up a working group to prepare the country for a flood of Polish returnees. Anecdotal evidence suggests the anticipated influx of returnees did not happen for two reasons (*Financial Times*, 2009r). First, some Polish migrants had moved abroad permanently and are now already well settled in host countries. Second, although some Polish migrants lost their jobs, they are still entitled to more generous benefits in host countries such as the UK (despite cuts in welfare entitlements) compared to what they would receive in Poland; therefore, they did not have much incentive to leave.

For Filipino workers, however, the reasons for return were somewhat different. The fear of non-renewal of contracts or the imposition of lower wages and inferior labour conditions under new contracts, especially in the Middle East, seem to have played an important role.

As in past recessions, a number of host countries were trying to encourage or persuade migrants to return home. At the end of 2008, Spain, for example, offered to pay for the air travel expenses of non-EU immigrants who were unemployed and eligible for unemployment benefits and their families. Spain also offered to pay non-EU immigrants their accumulated unemployment benefits in two lump sums (40% of the amount in Spain and 60% on returning home). The offer was subject to the condition that these immigrants will surrender their residence permits and work visas and stay away from Spain for three years, after which they will have priority for re-entry to the country. Only 20 countries with bilateral social security agreements with Spain were eligible (OECD, 2009: 41).

In 2009, Japan introduced a voluntary return programme offering payments of 300,000 yen for each *nikkeijin* adult (ethnic Japanese descendants of earlier Japanese migrants to Latin America), and 200,000 yen for each dependent who left the country and agreed not to return on the same visa. Concentrated in sectors seriously affected by the economic downturn, *nikkeijin* suffered from a much higher rate of unemployment (estimated at above 20%) than Japanese nationals. As of January 2010, more than 17,000 unemployed *nikkeijin* have returned to their home countries under the programme, but at least three times as many did so outside the programme, possibly to retain their eligibility to return to Japan.

In February 2009, the Czech Republic introduced a policy to pay EUR 500 and airfare to unemployed migrant workers. This move mainly targeted people from Mongolia, Uzbekistan and Viet Nam who had been legally employed as temporary contract workers before losing their jobs.

However, experience suggests that the impact of such incentives on return may not be very encouraging; it is often marginal and, in some cases, even perverse. In the mid-1970s, when West Germany offered incentive packages to encourage return in the wake of its ban on labour immigration, the move fuelled new entries through family reunification, and some immigrants, especially those from Turkey, who were used to circulatory movements, decided to stay put in Germany, eventually making it an immigration country.

The French programme of incentives launched during the same period did not have much success either. An important reason for this was that returnees were required to give up not only their residence and work permits but also their claims on social insurance benefits. Later, in 1977, the financial incentives were increased, but the response from the Algerian immigrants whom these incentives mainly targeted remained subdued. As in West Germany, instead of returning, many brought in their dependents, swelling family reunification flows. More than 60 per cent of the returnees were Spanish and Portuguese immigrants (Dustmann, 1996), and it was likely that, as conditions in their home countries improved, many of them would have returned anyway.

The results of the incentive programmes launched during the current crisis do not seem to be any more promising than those tried in the past. At the time of writing, the Spanish programme mentioned above had failed to elicit overwhelming response. By January 2010, only 10,000 unemployed immigrants had signed up and returned home, compared with some 137,000 persons who were eligible. The Czech programme was more successful. By March 2009, 74 per cent of Mongolian immigrants had already signed up for the programme. Although the response from the Uzbeks was much slower, the first phase of the programme was successfully completed with about 2,000 returnees.

In several countries, the recession has prompted policymakers to make declarations urging preferences for domestic workers over foreigners that could well serve as an indirect push for jobless immigrants to return home. As noted earlier, in April 2009, US Senator Grassley, for example, suggested that Microsoft should retrench foreign workers to protect American workers. In the UK, the Home Secretary declared in February 2009 that "it was right in a downturn...to do more to put British workers first." Labour strikes against legally employed Italian workers in UK oil refineries in March 2009 showed that political pressure was building up to push migrants to return home even though they came from a member state of the EU and were legally employed.

The public mood in many EU countries on the matter was not much different. A Harris/*Financial Times* poll conducted in April 2009 (referred to above) in five major EU member countries showed that the majority would like unemployed foreign workers from other EU countries to go back to their own countries. The recent trend (i.e. prior to the recession) towards restricting eligibility for social benefits, including those for temporary and irregular migrants, in several rich receiving countries could also be an added element favouring return.

As further discussed in the next chapter, the problem with precipitous return programmes driven by political pressures or sectarian interests and other short-term considerations is that they may well be counterproductive for the receiving countries themselves and for global economic recovery.

Return migration works well and is generally more sustainable when it is voluntary and, when needed, supported by well-planned assistance at both ends (Ghosh, ed., 2009a). However, return generally is voluntary only when conditions in the source country are sufficiently promising. More than the absolute level of income or development, it is often the rate of growth of the economy and future prospects – that is, the feeling that tomorrow will be a better day for a migrant and his or her family – that encourages a migrant's voluntary return (Ghosh, ed., 2009a). Return is also facilitated when the distance between the sending and receiving countries is short, the travel cost low and the migrant has the possibility of re-entering the host country with ease, as was the case with the Polish migrant workers in the UK mentioned earlier.

Entitlement to social benefits also plays an important part in return. In many countries, including the United States and the UK, recently arrived and irregular migrants are not eligible for most social benefits. However, for those migrants who are eligible, the non-portability of social benefits to the home country could be a major constraint on return. This applies particularly to migrants from developing countries that do not provide adequate social safety nets. This might be a reason why, despite the economic downturn, there was no immediate large-scale exodus of Mexicans living in the United States: the same number of migrants (450,000) returned to Mexico in 2008 as in 2007, although the situation may be changing, as noted in the next section.

When economic conditions are bad in both host countries and home countries, unemployed migrants may try to move to a third country, as was experienced in some of the previous crises. Given the global spread of the present crisis, however, such opportunities are almost non-existent, although there are some rare exceptions. As part of its efforts to meet its long-term skill shortages, the Canadian province of Alberta, for example, launched early in 2008 an information campaign to attract holders of H-1B and E-3 visas in the United States by offering them better facilities such as a faster and surer track to the permanent residence permit (OECD, 2009). As already noted, if recovery proves asymmetrical, with some of the emerging economies moving faster than the others, some of the migrants from these emerging economies may return home. These countries may also become potential new destinations for migrants from other countries.

2.3 Irregular migration: Conflicting trends

Will there be delayed reverse irregular return to host countries?

How will the crisis affect irregular migration? Economic crises impact irregular migration in different and, to some extent, conflicting ways. The present crisis is not likely to be any different. When economic conditions are bad and job opportunities dry up in the destination country, irregular migrants tend to stay away; more so if, as is likely, both border control and employer sanctions against employment of irregular migrants are tightened at the same time. Not surprisingly, flows of irregular migration from Mexico to the United States, for example, stopped rising in 2008, as was also the case during the recession of 2001–2002 (Passel and Cohn, 2008). In April 2009, the Pew Hispanic Center estimated that illegal crossings fell to 500,000 in 2008, compared with an average of 800,000 during 2002 and 2006. The number of people apprehended while trying to enter the United States illegally fell to 724,000 in 2008, the lowest level since 1973. The findings of a report by the US Department of Homeland Security seem to be consistent with this. It estimated that by January 2009, the stock of irregular migrants would have fallen to 10.8 million, from 11.8 million in January 2007 (Hoefer et al., 2010).

The US Department of Homeland Security attributed this decline to more effective border control, which raises costs and risks for potential immigrants. However, as Wayne Cornelius, emeritus director of the Center for Comparative Immigration Studies at the University of California, San Diego, argues, the economic downturn was probably a more important reason. For example, unemployment in the US state of California, which has long attracted and relied on cheap labour, had shot up to 11.6 per cent by the middle of 2009. Jobs were scarce and those still available were less stable. No wonder then that potential migrants were less willing to pay thousands of dollars to traffickers and risk their lives in the desert to migrate illegally. The same situation probably explains the sharp decline in US states such as Arizona (13%) and Florida (25%). True, Arizona had introduced tougher immigration controls, but if this was the main reason for the drop in the level of irregular migrants, it could not explain the sharper fall in Florida, which implemented no such measures (Chishti and Bergeron, 2010).

The size of the irregular migrant population in a particular state or region within a country may be influenced by other factors as well. For instance, as mentioned in the next section, in times of economic crisis, some irregular migrants in a given country may decide to move to states or areas already hosting large migrant communities for the support they could get from social networks, even if the job prospects in these locations are not sufficiently encouraging.

However, there are also opposing forces that tend to increase irregular migration during an economic crisis. One such risk concerns a rise in overstayers. Many unemployed workers with temporary, job-related visas would be unable to find new jobs in a recessionary environment either in the host country or in a new one. Even under the relatively liberal Swedish immigration policy, an unemployed migrant holding a work permit must find a job within three months from the date he/she became unemployed – not the date of expiry of the work permit – to avoid departure. Returning home may be costly, or the situation there may be even worse. The migrant may then be left with no other alternative than to go underground and try to find a job in the informal sector. It is difficult to say at this stage how many temporary migrants holding job-related visas might be driven to this situation by the present crisis. However, the danger is real, and surely it will be more so if the crisis becomes protracted and joblessness continues to remain at a high level.

A recessionary environment may also encourage new sources of irregular migration. As argued earlier, if the present restrictive trends towards migration gain further ground, it would take some time before they can be reversed even if output recovery starts in the meantime. In such a situation, some students and tourists may also decide to stay in the host country beyond the date of expiry of their respective visas in anticipation of taking up jobs when labour demand picks up following recovery. As for new irregular inflows, it is well known that when emigration pressure in source countries is high and there is unmet labour demand in destination countries, and especially when the two converge, restrictions on immigration only drive flows to irregular channels (Ghosh, 1998). If output recovery moves ahead and labour demand starts to pick up in destination countries but immigration restrictions persist, a similar situation is most likely to emerge in the wake of the crisis.

The most disquieting potential source of irregular migration lies in joblessness and rising poverty in labour-abundant origin countries. As discussed earlier, when a destination country faces an economic downturn, irregular immigration generally slows down. However, when economic woes spread to sending counties and pose threats to livelihoods and stability in sending countries, things can rapidly change.

Given the highly synchronized nature of the present crisis, the same can happen this time. With the rise in joblessness and poverty in poor countries, there is a real danger that migrants from these countries, especially those that have no social safety nets, could be propelled to seek escape in more affluent developed and developing countries. One study suggested that if real wages in Mexico were to fall by 10 per cent, the United States can face a rise of between 6.4 per cent and 8.7 per cent in attempted irregular entry (Hanson and Spilimbergo, 1999). If the present crisis becomes protracted and conditions further deteriorate in poor countries, some of the erstwhile returnees may also join irregular outflows, staging a delayed reverse return to rich countries.

Despite the small decline in Mexican migration to the United States in September 2009, as mentioned above, a Pew Research Center survey revealed that 31 per cent of Mexicans would like to migrate to the United States, and more than half of them would do so even without authorization (Pew Research Center, 2009b). For many Mexicans, the troubled economy was a major problem, alongside crime and illegal drugs. In fact, press reports in January 2010 were already suggesting a surge in the number of Mexicans trying to cross illegally to the United States by sea. Indicative of this trend was the rise in the total number of interdictions at sea, including those related to drugs and human smuggling, to 419 in fiscal year 2009, compared with 224 in 2008 and 134 in 2007 (*The New York Times*, 2010c). With the pressure for irregular migration thus building up, human traffickers could have a field day and see their trade flourish, unless remedial measures are taken (this is discussed further in the next chapter).

As for the stock of irregular migrants, there are also reasons (discussed below) why some of the existing migrants holding job-related temporary visas may decide to go underground upon losing their jobs and thus add to the irregular stock, although the numbers involved may be limited.

2.4 Internal movements

Escape to rural areas, urban informal sectors and social support hubs

The recession has also led to an increase in internal movements in both rich and poor countries. An important reason for this is that, in the absence of social safety nets or income-support alternatives, jobless migrants move back to rural areas or move to urban centres in search of informal jobs. For migrants holding job-related temporary visas who have become unemployed, such movement also provides relative safety from detection and deportation on grounds of their irregular status. In countries where the level of unemployment varies widely from one area to another, many people move in search of jobs or to gain support from their social networks in less-affected areas. In China, for example, in 2008, many migrants in export centres in the southern parts of the country returned home to rural areas after production was scaled down. However, in Beijing and inland cities where migrant workers were already more prevalent in the construction and services sectors, arrivals continued to rise (*Financial Times*, 2009ai).

In some developing countries, the opening up of the interior and industrial relocation in the hinterland can influence criss-cross internal movements. The economic crisis has been contributing to this process in China. As factories in coastal areas move to poorer regions in western China to take advantage of lower wages and taxes, local workers could now find jobs closer to home, leading to a decline in previous movements from these areas.

However, as export orders were rising with the economic recovery, factories in the urban-industrial areas of Guandong that shed workers in 2008–2009 were already worried about labour shortages. Some tried to adapt to the new situation by turning to temporary workers as a short-term shot in the arm, while provincial authorities raised the minimum wages for these urban and industrial centres. Eventually, some of the vacant positions could be expected to attract unemployed workers from other parts of the country, leading to new internal movements (discussed in further detail in chapter 5).

Migrants, especially those who are young and single, are generally more mobile than the local population. However, in countries such as the United States (which, even in normal times, has a much higher rate of internal mobility than, for example, Western Europe), the recession seems to have also generated some new mobility from one state to another for the local population, depending on the relative employment situation.

Earlier census reports in the United States suggested that the recession was contributing to the lack of mobility, as Americans stayed in homes they could not sell. Figures released by the Census Bureau in December 2009 (reflecting the situation as of July 2009) similarly indicated that states in southern and western United States that had attracted large numbers of people during the real estate boom a few years ago were experiencing sharply lower growth in population. States like Arizona, Nevada and Florida that used to lead the country in internal immigration were now low on the list. At the same time, however, some states, including Florida, Nevada and California, saw more Americans moving out than coming in, contributing to internal mobility. Among migrants, too, internal movement patterns were shifting. Census data showed that the once-hectic flows of Hispanic migrants to "bubble towns" such as Las Vegas and Phoenix, as well as to parts of the Midwest, had slowed. However, traditional migrant heartlands such as California saw an increase in Hispanics, as people turned to their social networks for support.

2.5 Global migrant stock

How will the criss-cross of migration flows affect the global migrant stock?

Recession affects migration flows and reshapes both current and future migrant stock. Since, as discussed, new migration, from all indications, is slowing down, the rate of growth in migrant stock should also decelerate if other things do not change. To the extent that the downturn in host countries leads to a higher rate of return to home countries than in the past, it will also play a part in reducing the migrant stock or at least in decelerating its growth. It is difficult to anticipate what the net effect of these different, in-and-out movements on migrant stock is likely to be in the future; much would depend on the duration of the downturn and the shape of recovery, notably job and income recovery, and the country-specific situation.

Tentative estimates are available for a few countries, however. In the UK, it is projected that the migrant population will be smaller by some 360,000 by 2015, as compared with the pre-recession projection in July 2008, and will reduce the UK labour force by 200,000 (UK Department for Communities and Local Government, 2009). Short-term projections can be made on the basis of trends in flows in the coming years. For example, in Ireland, it was estimated that a net outflow of 60,000 occurred in the year ending April 2009; a further net outflow of 40,000 is forecast for the year ending April 2011. As for the current stock of working-age migrant population, the OECD estimated that a number of its member countries – Austria, France, Germany, the Netherlands and the United States – experienced declines in stock and negative net migration between 2008 and 2009 (OECD, 2010a).

In the event of a protracted crisis or a highly asymmetrical recovery with many poor sending countries lagging behind, the likelihood is that return migration to source countries will slow down, and new migration, mostly through irregular channels, as already argued, will increase, although actual entry will depend on the degree of effectiveness of border control. In a number of OECD countries, a net increase in entry through family reunification and humanitarian channels may also contribute to the total migrant stock, but many may not belong to the working-age group.

However, given that annual flows are quite small relative to total stocks, in most cases, the changes in annual flows, as discussed above, will have a limited effect on the size of the migrant stocks, at least in the short term. More than the number, it is the changing composition and characteristics of the migrant stock (including newly arrived migrants) that deserves closer attention as they raise some serious policy concerns. This is taken up in the following sections.

The downturn can make more migrants go underground with an irregular status

As already noted, despite a slight temporary decline in the stock of irregular migrants in countries such as the United States, there are signs that the pressure for new migration through irregular channels is building up. No less disquietingly, the delay in job recovery could make some of the existing legal migrants go underground. In case of dismissal, migrants who are on job-related visas have three options: (a) return home or go to a third country where there may still be some opportunities; (b) look for alternative jobs in less-affected sectors in host countries, mostly at lower wages and with less social protection; and (c) go underground and try to eke out a living in the informal sector. However, given the internal and external spread of the present crisis, the possibilities under both (a) and (b) remain quite limited; these are also not without risks (this will be discussed in the next chapter). The probability is that many of the sacked temporary workers will add to the number of new irregular inflows of migrants and inflate, however modestly, the total irregular migrant stock.

Another change in the composition of stock concerns skilled migrants. Despite recession-led cutbacks in skilled immigration, in some cases, most receiving countries, especially in the industrial world, remained anxious to benefit from new skills and innovation. When recovery starts to gather pace, they will face a still more urgent need for new and additional skills to facilitate the process of industrial restructuring and improve capital productivity. Indeed, the speed of recovery itself in certain sectors would largely depend on such restructuring. Despite some recent cutbacks in skilled immigration, as noted earlier, in general, these countries would therefore be less keen to reduce new inflows of skilled migrants more than inflows of low-skilled ones. Also, defying populist pressure, both governments and companies were already devising special schemes or arrangements to maintain, as far as possible, skilled personnel on the payroll. To put it differently, skilled migrants were most likely to receive preferential treatment in receiving countries in relation to both new flows and those who are already on the payroll.[20] However, this slight new tilt in favour of skilled migrants will have at best only a marginal impact on the ratio of skilled migrants to low-skilled ones in migrant stocks as a whole. This is because low-skilled migrants by far constitute a larger part of existing stocks.

A crisis brings changes in labour markets that often affect migrant and non-migrant populations differently

Just as a crisis brings change in the composition of migrant stocks (including new migrants) in terms of their legal status in the host country, it also reshapes the distribution of migrant and non-migrant workers between sectors and their labour market characteristics, including, as mentioned, their skill composition. It is important to note that while most of these changes have an impact on the total workforce, migrants and non-migrants are not necessarily affected in the same way.

In rich countries, job losses were particularly severe in the male-dominated industries of construction, finance and manufacturing. In the United States, for example, between the end of 2008 and the middle of 2009, job openings declined by 47 per cent in manufacturing, 37 per cent in construction and 22 per cent in retail. In general, immigrants in rich countries had a disproportionate presence in these most-affected sectors, and they were therefore the worse sufferers. This might have led to a shift in the occupations of migrants to less affected and, in many cases, less attractive, sectors, including agriculture, as had happened in Spain; in some countries, such as the Czech Republic and Italy, many migrants opted for self-employment. The fact that immigrants are generally more mobile than local workers has helped the process. This probably also helps to explain why migrant employment has held up relatively well in a number of OECD countries, especially in sectors such as education, health and domestic services.

The concentration of immigrants in sectors more sensitive to economic fluctuations is not the only reason why migrants tend to suffer more from

[20] As discussed earlier in this chapter, this has prevented a number of receiving countries from putting severe curbs on new admission of skilled workers, although the definition of skilled workers has been tightened.

joblessness than nationals. There are at least three other important reasons for this:

First, many migrants hold temporary jobs which are often the first to be cut. They also generally have less secure contractual arrangements which are easier and less costly to terminate. Based on data from past recessions, the OECD estimated that the cyclical sensitivity of temporary jobs is twice that of total employment (OECD, 2010b). There was a high concentration of migrants in temporary jobs in most OECD countries. Their share in temporary employment exceeded that of the nationals by 50 per cent or more in a number of these countries; in Spain, almost 48 per cent of migrants were on temporary contracts in 2008.

Compared to nationals, migrants in many OECD countries tend to have a shorter tenure on the job, on average. This makes them more vulnerable to retrenchment during an economic crisis. Data collected by OECD revealed such a difference between migrants and nationals in a number of countries, including Austria, Belgium, Portugal and the UK, and particularly in Ireland, Spain and Finland. As of 2008, in Ireland and Spain, for example, between one third and one fourth of migrant workers had been recruited in the previous 12 months, compared with 15 per cent for nationals.

Second, as already noted, in times of economic downturn, employers can try to save on labour costs by shedding jobs, but they can also do so by reducing the number of hours worked. Such labour hoarding is useful to companies as it helps them avoid loss of human and social capital and new recruitment and training costs. The schemes are therefore mostly applicable to permanent workers. Since a high proportion of migrant workers hold temporary jobs, they are less likely to be covered by these labour hoarding schemes. The adjustment to lower labour demand in these cases tends to take the form of retrenchment, contributing to increased joblessness among migrant workers. Another reason may well be the skill composition of immigrant workers. In most OECD countries, immigrants are over-represented among low-skilled workers. They are more vulnerable because their productivity is low and, in most cases, they can be more easily replaced. There is enough empirical evidence to confirm this; see for example, Davis et al. (1996) and Hoynes (1999).

Finally, the selective layoff of migrant workers may also be influenced by prejudices and discrimination against migrants especially when anti-immigrant feeling runs high and the protection of labour rights of migrants is weak (this is further discussed in the next chapter).

The recession will also have an effect on labour force composition in terms of gender and age. In many rich countries, the worst-affected industries, as mentioned above, were male-dominated. In the United States, nine in every 10 construction workers were male, as were seven in every 10 manufacturing workers. Not surprisingly, in the United States, though men made up half of the workforce, they accounted for over three quarters of job losses since the recession began. In the past, the rates of male and female unemployment were about the same.

In Ireland, the unemployment rate for male workers increased from 4.8 per cent to 9.3 per cent, while for female workers, the rate rose from 4.3 per cent to 5.5 per cent between the second quarter of 2007 and the fourth quarter of 2008.

As immigrant women entered the labour market in many of these countries to help compensate for the income losses of male family members, there was an increase in their participation rate in Canada, the United States and the member states of the EU-15 (OECD, 2010a). However, in most OECD countries, unemployment among foreign-born women increased at a rate slower than that for their male counterparts.

In emerging and developing countries, women, including female migrants, were more vulnerable in labour-intensive and export-oriented sectors such as clothing and garment-making, footwear and food processing, as well as microchips and electronic products. In these countries, female workers, including the female migrants engaged in these sectors, were more vulnerable.

The crisis has had an impact on the gender distribution of the workforce between sectors. In countries such as the United States, as men lost their jobs in the worst-affected sectors, many of them looked for low-wage, and often less stable, jobs in sectors hitherto dominated by female workers such as health care and education. This in some cases affected the competitive position of female workers, both domestic and foreign. Also, since women earn, on average, 20 per cent less than men, families that solely rely on income that women bring in faced financial strain (this is further discussed in the next chapter). Acceptance of lower wages and other conditions, probably conflated with female migrants' increased labour force participation rates mentioned above, also helped to increase their numbers in the job market.

As for non-migrant female workers, just as the downturn was pushing some of them out of work, it was also driving some women back to the workforce. In the United States, for example, some of the educated women who had left work to stay at home were driven back to the job market, either because their husbands were laid off or had fears of being laid off, or because of their falling fortunes due to cuts in their husbands' salaries or a decline in the value of their investments (*The New York Times*, 2009f).

It is difficult to indicate the extent to which the shift is likely to affect male workers. However, in the United States, the Bureau of Labor Statistics found that among women with a college education, aged between 25 and 44 years, and living with a spouse, the proportion of those who were working or looking for work increased to 78.4 per cent in the first half of 2009 from 76 per cent in the same period in 2007. The proportion of men in the same age group and with similar labour market characteristics declined slightly from 97.4 per cent to 97.1 per cent during the same period. In any case, these shifts in the labour market are not expected to have more than a marginal effect, if any, on migrant workers.

While the rise in unemployment in rich countries affected all age groups, the fastest increases in most cases (as in the United States) were among those between 60 and 64 years and those between 20 and 24 years. On the other hand, there is evidence that some of the older people who had retired were driven back to the workforce because of the economic downturn.

Among the migrant groups particularly affected by the crisis were young migrants. While youth unemployment was a serious problem for both migrant and non-migrant populations, conditions were much tougher for foreign-born youths in countries such as Denmark, Ireland and Spain. In Ireland, the employment rate for young immigrants aged 15–24 years dropped by 15 percentage points between 2008 and 2009, almost twice the figure for non-migrants. As of 2009, the unemployment rate for foreign-born individuals aged 15–24 years had reached 15 per cent in the United States, 20 per cent in Canada, and 24 per cent, on average, in the EU; in Spain, the figure was as high as 41 per cent (OECD, 2010a).

Changes in age composition and participation rates in the labour market affect the overall employment/unemployment situation. However, when these changes run in opposite directions for migrants and non-migrants, they are also affected differently. An increase in employment can very well coexist with a higher rate of unemployment when the increase in employment falls short of the increase in the working-age population and in labour market participation rates.

The working-age migrant population in a number of OECD countries fell during the recession; the rate of migrant unemployment in these countries would have been higher had the proportion of the working-age group remained constant or increased. Several other countries that saw an increase in migrant employment also experienced an increase in the migrant population aged 15–64 years between 2008 and 2009; the increase in total employment thus had little effect in lowering the migrant unemployment rate. On the other hand, the ageing of the local population in several OECD countries led to a decline in the number of persons of working age. The lower participation rate among the local population kept their unemployment rate lower but showed a decline in their total employment. In comparing the unemployment situation of migrants and non-migrants in a given country, it is therefore important to take into account the changes in the demographics and participation rates of the two groups.

As will be further discussed in this study, the rise in youth unemployment among migrants, combined with the changes in the labour market characteristics of total migration flows to rich countries – including a relative increase in the number of entries through family reunification and humanitarian channels that suggest a low employment outcome – will continue to be a source of concern in the coming years.

Recession-driven changes in the configuration of international migration and the composition of the workforce, affecting both nationals and migrants, as discussed in this chapter, help us to better understand their economic, social and political effects on countries rich and poor. These effects are analysed in the next chapter.

3. Effects of changes in the migration pattern: Discerning perils and pitfalls

The effects of recession-driven changes in the configuration of migration and the composition of the workforce could be manifold and mostly disturbing for both rich and poor countries. Some analysts have argued that these effects are temporary and that over the medium to long term, migration flows would remain unaffected by the recession. According to these analysts, flows would continue to be shaped by structural factors, including labour market and demographic asymmetry between countries, and future trends affecting the world economy. This may be largely true. And yet, as already discussed, some of the seemingly short-term effects on migration and the policy responses to them could have an enduring effect, as was experienced in the years following the Great Depression. Also, as noted, rising youth unemployment among migrants, combined with an increase (relative to labour migrants) in the flows of non-working-age migrants and of those with low employment outcome due to entry through family reunification and refugee channels, as has been the experience in a number of OECD countries during the present crisis, could have long-lasting consequences.

Admittedly, the depth of these effects themselves, and at least in some cases even the degree of probability of them taking place, would largely depend not just on the shape of future recovery, but also on the nature of the response of migration policies nations might develop at both ends of the flows. This chapter discusses some of the potential perils and pitfalls of the recession-driven changes in migration, and how perverse or deficient migration policies can aggravate them.

3.1 Effects on host countries

Indiscriminate restrictions on immigration can harm future growth and retard recovery

Economic slowdown reduces labour demand. It would thus be normal for a receiving country to reduce new immigration consistent with changes in the labour market. However, when a receiving country takes draconian measures to impose undue and indiscriminate restrictions on immigration due to panic or populist political pressure, these measures are likely to place a heavy discount on its long-term growth.

Several studies have shown the links between immigration and economic growth.[21] In April 2009, an official study in the UK suggested that an estimated fall in the migrant stock by around 360,000 by 2015, and a consequent reduction in the labour force by 200,000, would lead to a 0.1–0.125 per cent decline in the country's economic growth (UK Department of Communities and Local Government, 2009). Another study carried out by Christian Dustmann, a professor at University College London, using data over four years since 2004, found that immigrants from the eight countries that joined the EU in 2004 (A8 countries) contributed significantly more to the UK tax and benefit system than they received. A detailed analysis by the UK Home Office on the fiscal impact of immigration came to a similar conclusion. It estimated that, in 1999–2000, migrants in the UK made a net fiscal contribution of approximately GBP 28.8 billion (Gott and Johnston, 2002).

Research presented to the EU Parliament showed that migrants from within the EU had boosted the region's aggregate GDP by 0.28 per cent since 2004. Calculations for Germany showed that if the aggregate net payments made by the immigrant population were evenly distributed among future-born Germans, their net tax burden would fall by about 30 per cent, assuming a constant annual immigration inflow of 0.25 per cent of the initial resident population (Bonin et al., 2000). In Italy, Unioncamare, a business association, estimated that migrants produce 9 per cent of the country's GDP (*Financial Times*, 2009l). While they account for one out of 10 total workers, many do not have their families with them, reducing the Italian economy's social burden. Clearly, though, immigration cannot provide a long-term solution to the fiscal problem of an ageing population.[22]

Such potential gains are foregone when a country takes knee-jerk measures and puts sudden brakes on migration; worse still, these actions carry the risk of causing serious economic and social dislocation. In the United States, census data analysed for 25 metropolitan areas by the Fiscal Policy Institute in New York showed a close link (though not necessarily a causal relationship) between economic growth in urban areas and immigration. As David Kallick, director of immigration research at the Institute put it: "Economic growth in urban areas has been clearly connected with an increase in immigrants' share of the local labour force" (*The New York Times*, 2010f).[23]

[21] There have been a number of studies on the economic benefits of freer movement of workers from developing to developed countries (e.g. Hamilton and Whaley, 1984; Rodrik, 2002; World Bank, 2005). These studies bring into focus possible welfare gains from a more efficient allocation of labour. However, they do not take into account all the relevant economic and social costs involved in such cross-border movements. See Ghosh (2005), Chapter 8, pp. 163–164.

[22] This is because, over time, immigrants generally tend to imbibe the cultural mores of the host society and their birth rate declines in line with that of the local population.

[23] See also FPI (2010).

A drastic or unwarranted ban on inflows of foreign workers can also encourage tit-for-tat retaliation. The consequences could be serious for two reasons. First, since more and more countries – one fourth of nearly 100 countries covered in a 1999 ILO survey[24] – are major senders and major receivers of migrants at the same time, the potential scope for such retaliation is quite considerable. Second, retaliatory action may not necessarily be confined to movement of people; it may extend to other economic flows such as trade and investment, and some countries may find it more expedient to use their superior leverage in these latter areas, fuelling wider mutually destructive protectionism. It may even cause or increase inter-state political tension.

Laying off migrants or persuading them to return to make room for national workers does not work automatically, nor is it necessarily cost-effective. Much depends on the availability of an adequate number of nationals with the necessary skills, as well as a willingness to take on, under similar conditions, jobs held by migrants. To illustrate, during the 1998 Asian financial crisis, the Thai government had to backtrack on a plan to substitute Thais for migrants in rice mills. In 2008, fewer than 120 Thais responded to advertisements for 150,000 fisheries-related workers in Samut Sakhon province (Martin, 2009). In the UK, the proportion of foreign workers in small and medium enterprises rose to 48 per cent in 2008. However, in 2009, 29 per cent of employers were worried that foreign personnel would return home, while 40 per cent said that they would have to shed labour due to the economic downturn. At the same time, a Home Office spokesman announced that "government and independent research continue to find no significant evidence of negative employment effects from migration" (*Telegraph*, 2008). This seems to cast doubt on any direct correlation between indiscriminate immigration restrictions or encouraged return of immigrants and better labour market prospects for local workers.

Why the loss of skilled workers could be particularly harmful for innovation and growth

Unduly restricting inflows of new skills or reducing the existing pool of such resources could be particularly harmful. Normally, in times of economic downturn, employers try to delay shedding their skilled personnel not just because they are scarce relative to unskilled or semi-skilled workers, but also because they could be of help in cutting costs through the introduction of new methods and systems as part of the adjustment to the economic downturn. Employers may also wish to hoard them in the hope that when the recession

[24] "Major" is defined as including only countries whose labour market or gross national product (GNP) was affected to an extent of at least 1 per cent by international labour migrants, disregarding asylum-seekers and refugees.

ends, the company would remain competitive and would be able to take full advantage of the opportunities opened up by the recovery, while avoiding the direct and indirect costs of new recruitment.

However, these considerations lose much of their weight when a recession portends to be long and the future looks uncertain. This indeed is the kind of situation that seems to have developed in many migrant-receiving industrial countries, especially since the last quarter of 2008. As indicated in chapter 2, continuing uncertainty about the depth and duration of the crisis has led several countries to reduce new inflows of skilled personnel. Some companies have introduced large-scale retrenchment and, in many cases, the axe has fallen on skilled personnel as well. In Germany, engineering companies, which form the backbone of the country's export-dependent economy, were expected to shed as many as 25,000 skilled workers in 2009 as result of a sharp fall in orders that followed a long, five-year boom in the sector, when production rose 40 per cent and more than 100,000 jobs were created (*Financial Times*, 2009f).[25]

Immigrant workers holding temporary contracts have been exposed to the risk of becoming the first casualties. In the United States, for example, even companies in skill-intensive technical sectors have come under political pressure, as reflected in US Senator Grassley's call for Microsoft to shed foreign, rather than national, workers, and his urging for curbs on H-1B temporary visas (discussed in chapter 2).

As a knee-jerk reaction to the recession, manufacturing companies in the United States shed more than 2 million jobs in 2008–2009. However, with economic recovery gradually gathering pace, many companies were facing shortages of engineers and other skilled workers for jobs that required knowledge of mathematics and the ability to read technical blueprints. The ageing of the existing workforce was making the situation worse. About 19 per cent of US manufacturing workers were aged 54 years or older, and only 7 per cent of workers were under 25 years of age. At the aircraft manufacturer Boeing, 40 per cent of the labour force (60,000 workers) would be eligible to retire by 2015, and the company was worried about how it would meet its labour needs (*Financial Times*, 2010b).

A shortage of skilled engineers was threatening to limit oil supply growth in the coming three to five years, as the greying industry was unable to recruit, train and maintain the engineers needed to meet the demands of new drilling projects, according to Andrew Gould, chairman and chief executive

[25] Comments by Manfred Wittenstein, head of VDMA, an engineering organization.

officer of Schlumberger, the world's biggest oil services company. "The only kit that is really, really difficult to get is the human kit," he said (*Financial Times*, 2008a). Companies in most industrial countries, notably the United States, have in the past vastly benefited from skilled migrant inflows. Cypress Semiconductor Corporation reported that about 40 per cent of its research and development jobs were held by skilled migrants and that each job created nine additional jobs (Migration News, 1997). Two thirds of Silicon Valley companies were started by people not born in the United States.

It is not without significance that in the 2010 Intel Science Talent Search, a national contest that identifies and honours top mathematics and science high school students in America based on their solutions to scientific problems, the majority of the 40 finalists were of immigrant origin, mostly Chinese and Indians (*The New York Times*, 2010e).

In Italy, where an estimated 165,000 businesses are run by foreign entrepreneurs, tripling the number since 2005, the economy has been benefiting from the innovative and entrepreneurial spirit of immigrants. As Massimo Canovi, a director of MoneyGram, a US-based money transfer company, put it: "Immigrant entrepreneurs have an edge over Italians, who see the crisis as an insurmountable obstacle. They have a different mentality and approach. They fight for the future, while we [Italians] are anchored to the past and stuck in traditional schemes" (*Financial Times*, 2009l). Mr Canovi may have been a little effusive, but the distinctive entrepreneurial contribution of immigrants remains a reality. In Germany, engineering companies still reeling from the economic crisis were facing a skills shortage that threatened to undermine the sector's long-term recovery. Willi Fuchs, head of the German engineering association VDI, said that even in 2009, when the sector saw its sales drop by a quarter, there had been a shortage of 34,000 engineers. Prognos, a research institute, estimated that the country's job market would be short of almost 3 million professionals by 2015 (*Financial Times*, 2010h).

A study by William Kerr of Harvard Business School showed that nearly 40 per cent of patents filed in 2005 by Intel, a silicon chip maker, were for work done by people of Chinese or Indian origin (*The Economist*, 2009a). Although some of these people are US-born children of earlier migrants, most of these innovations seem to have taken place over time from migration.

Mr Kerr also found that the share of all patents given to scientists of Chinese and Indian origin more than tripled from 4.1 per cent in the second half of the 1970s to 13.9 per cent between 2000 and 2004. However, the share of patents awarded to US-born scientists fell between 1975 and 2004. Does the better performance of immigrants also imply that they are simply crowding out US-born scientists? On the contrary, another study, jointly by William Kerr and William Lincoln (2008) of the University of Michigan,[26] showed that instead of displacing US-born scientists, the inflow of H-1B workers may have also helped the former's work. This is supported by the fact that when the US government increased the number of H-1B entrants by 10 per cent, total patents increased by 2 per cent; and though mostly awarded to immigrants, the share of US-born scientists in the award of new patents also increased. The interchange of ideas and feedback of knowledge may have been the main reason.

As already noted, given the nature and depth of industrial decline especially in manufacturing, recovery will call for considerable industrial restructuring, with a shift, for example, to new "industrial services" that are linked to manufacturing (e.g. maintenance, upkeep and modernization, as well as operating equipment and machinery) and have higher profit margins (*Financial Times*, 2010f).[27] Skilled immigration could be an important source of the new skills and talents, as well as the dynamism and innovative spirit, needed to meet the urgent need.

Not surprisingly, sources close to the international labour market were already worried that some companies in advanced economies had been using the blunt instrument of cutting staff across the board and that a talent shortage in these economies could worsen when the economic upturn arrives. As Jeff Joerres, chief executive of Manpower, one of the world's biggest recruitment agencies, put it: "We are competing against the nightlife and the energy in Mumbai and Bangalore. This is a global labour market. If you see migration [of skilled people] back to Mexico, India [and] China, some of the Western countries could be really adversely impacted by a brain drain that they did not quite anticipate" (*Financial Times*, 2009j). His remarks were echoed by several other company managers. According to a leading European industrialist, a dearth of engineers in Europe would force companies to recruit heavily from emerging economies such as China and India in the future, leading to a big shift towards these countries (*Financial Times*, 2009s).[28] The problem, however, turns complex in as much as companies in emerging markets themselves have been complaining about a shortage of skills in some of the same sectors or the same types of skill.

[26] See also Agrawal et al. (2008).

[27] Armin Schmiedeberg at Bain Consultants recently estimated that these services for engineering products yielded a profit margin of 21 per cent – up to four times higher than that achieved by selling these goods.

[28] Comments by Benoit Poitier, chief executive of Air Liquide, an industrial bellwether supplying most industries with gas.

When depletion of the migrant stock leads to a decline in growth or hampers local-level development

Although at this stage of the crisis, it is difficult to foresee the exact situation, the discussion in chapter 2 suggested the possibility that with a slowdown in new immigration flows and an increase in return flows, many receiving countries could experience a depletion of their migrant stocks. Could this lead to a decline in the economic growth of receiving countries? As already noted, studies in the UK and the EU have shown that depletion of migrant stocks could have a negative effect on economic growth.

The net effect of changes in the migrant stock on a country's rate of growth would vary, depending on a number of factors, such as the composition of the migrant stock and the country-specific situation, including labour needs, and the costs involved in hosting and integrating immigrants.

As regards the skill composition of the migrant stock, an interesting point has emerged from a study on immigration (referred to in chapter 2) conducted by the New York-based Fiscal Policy Institute in 25 of the largest metropolitan areas in the United States. It showed that while all the areas benefited from increased immigration, the fastest economic growth was in cities such as Atlanta, Denver and Phoenix that received large influxes of immigrants with a mix of occupations and skills, and not the ones that drew primarily high-skilled, high-earning immigrants. However, it is difficult to say whether the skills mix alone was responsible for the differences in growth rates or whether other factors were also involved.

There is little doubt, however, that an essential condition of growth is the availability of a mix of skills needed across occupations and sectors of the economy; this includes low-level skills (FPI, 2009). In the UK, a plan to impose a cap on immigration from non-EU countries has led to protests from companies on grounds that this would be harmful to Britain's competitiveness and upsetting to its trading partners. Some companies said that "if they are going to make it hard for us, we'll just go offshore."[29]

As for the total migrant stock, one thing is clear: in areas where local economies or principal industries are largely dependent on migrants, their sudden and massive departure can cause serious economic and social dislocation. For instance, in the wake of the recession, the outflows of Nikkei Brazilians from Oizumu, north-west of Tokyo, were having a devastating effect on the local economy (*Financial Times*, 2009h). In the United States, reduced immigration

[29] Caron Pope at Cameron McKenna, cited in *Financial Times*, 30 July 2010.

and border crossings from Mexico were badly affecting the Latino economy in California, especially in cities like Chula Vista. Many businesses that used to cater to the immigrant population were closing down or striving just to stay afloat (*Financial Times*, 2009k).

When escape from joblessness means loss of skills and welfare: A painful trade-off

With the recession turning increasingly severe, many employers tried to save jobs by lowering conditions of work and wages through short-time schemes, unpaid staff leave and the like. As mentioned, several European governments, including, in particular, Germany and France, were financially supporting short-shift schemes. Even if these various schemes help avoid job shedding, they often imply lower earnings and/or other conditions of work. All workers involved suffer, but migrant workers and those from other vulnerable groups generally suffer the most.[30] The same applies to situations when sacked workers themselves are obliged to seek lower-level jobs or swell the ranks of the informal sector.

In many OECD countries (e.g. Denmark, Norway, Sweden and the UK), health and social services immigrants constitute 15 per cent of all immigrant workers. As these sectors were less affected by the crisis, they were also more likely to attract laid-off workers who would seek lower-level jobs in them. Even in normal times, it is not rare for migrants to accept lower-level jobs. Just like many Poles in the UK, Ukrainians in Poland often find themselves in hard and low-wage jobs that locals avoid, such as low-skilled construction work, fruit picking and farming, and domestic services. Not infrequently, these jobs are beneath their skills, due to lack of opportunities for Ukrainian immigrants or non-recognition of their professional diplomas. A study by Barrett and Kelly (2010) showed that, in times of boom in Ireland, the labour market disadvantage which immigrants experienced took the form of lower wages and occupational downgrading; in the recession, this was manifested in more rapid job losses (see next section). However, increased unemployment did not exclude downgrading of conditions for some of those who could retain their jobs.

The crisis is likely to aggravate this problem of "de-skilling" or occupational downgrading, especially since many migrants might actually be lacking the relevant skills for high-level jobs in the more resilient sectors (mentioned

[30] A discussed earlier, a large proportion of labour migrants hold temporary contracts and also have short tenure. In many cases, they are therefore excluded from these short work schemes and face outright retrenchment. Even those migrants who are covered may have to accept lower wages and working conditions under new contracts due to their weaker bargaining position.

further in the section below). In the United States, men, both nationals and migrants, were seeking to enter the low-wage but more stable jobs that the women had, such as retail services, home health care and babysitting – but a lot of them did not have adequate social protection. A disquieting impact of the recession in these cases is the fall-off in health insurance coverage.

A recession can encourage discrimination against migrants and other vulnerable groups

When economic distress strikes a country, migrants and those belonging to other vulnerable groups generally find themselves in a disadvantaged position relative to the rest of the society. This is often reflected in the areas of jobs and wages. Migrants, especially the temporary ones, are generally among the first to lose their jobs. Often paid less than the value of their net contribution to production, they also see a sharper fall in their incomes compared to the locals during downturns. A field survey carried out by the ILO in a number of industrial countries prior to the recession showed widespread discrimination against migrants and ethnic workers. For instance, more than one third of tested vacancies for semi-skilled jobs were closed to young male applicants of migrant or ethnic minority origin (ILO, 2004). The recent recession seems to have worsened the situation.

In the United States, since the recession started in December 2007, unemployment for immigrants has been rising faster than the general population. Estimates by Pew Research Center suggest that in the third quarter of 2007, the unemployment rate for immigrants was 4.1 per cent lower than that for native-born Americans (see Figure 5). However, by the third quarter of 2009, the situation had changed: unemployment among Americans had reached 9.5 per cent, while the rate for immigrants rose to 10 per cent. Among 50 per cent of the population of foreign-born Hispanics, the unemployment rate hit as high as 11.5 per cent (*Financial Times*, 2009ab). In Ireland, there was a fall in unemployment of total migrants between 2006 and 2007, and the rates of unemployment for migrants and non-migrants converged. However, by the beginning of 2009, there was a rapid divergence in unemployment as joblessness among migrants rose; the gap exceeded 5 percentage points in the first two quarters of 2009 (*Financial Times*, 2009ab). Unemployment data by sector also showed that the higher rates of job losses for migrants were not solely the result of their concentration in vulnerable sectors.

Figure 5: Differentiated impact on migrants and non-migrants (unemployment)

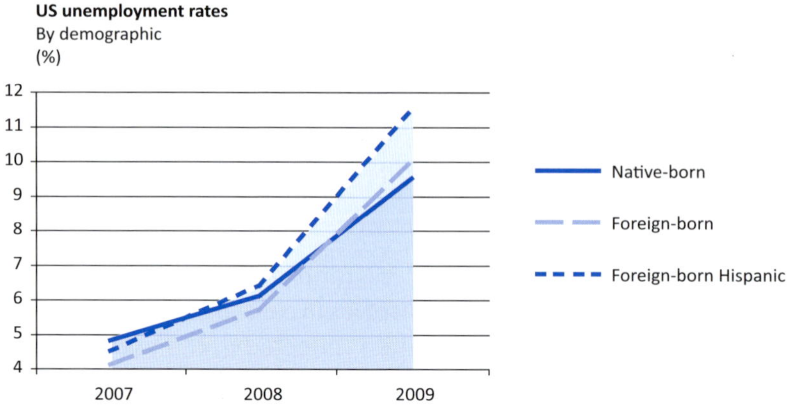

Source: Kochhar, 2008a.

A similar trend was discernible for other disadvantaged groups. Figures issued by the US Department of Labor for October 2009 showed that while unemployment was 13.1 per cent among Hispanics and 17.1 per cent among African Americans, it was 9.5 per cent among white Americans (see Figure 6). Although figures for December 2009 showed a slight fall in overall unemployment, these groups continued to be hit particularly hard, with unemployment reaching 12.6 per cent for Latinos and 16.5 per cent for African Americans, compared with 9 per cent for white Americans.

Figure 6: Unemployment trends by demographic group

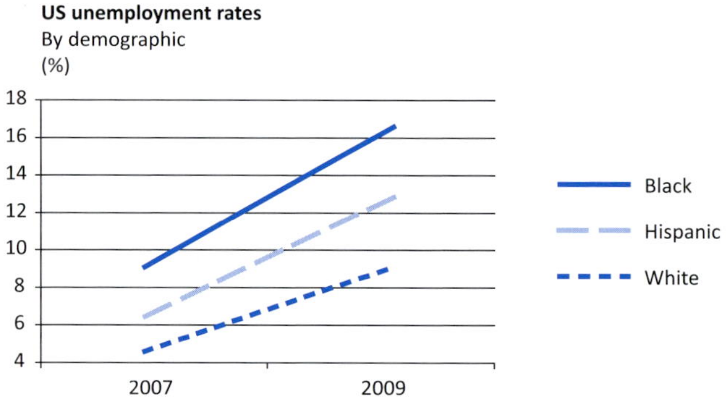

Source: Shierholz, 2010.

The employment situation in specific industries or sectors revealed a similar trend. For instance, a survey by the Pew Research Center showed that, at the end of 2006, the gap in unemployment rates for Hispanics and non-Hispanics in the US construction industry had shrunk to a meagre 0.5 per cent. However, by the first quarter of 2008, due mainly to the recession, the unemployment rate for Hispanics rose to 6.5 per cent, well above the 4.7 per cent rate for all non-Hispanics. Also, significantly, within the Latino group, foreign-born Latinos were worse off than the US-born ones (Kochhar, 2008b).

Another Pew Research Center survey in January 2009 revealed that more than 63 per cent of Hispanics thought that economic conditions were poor, compared to 59 per cent of the general population. Similar differences were found between the shares of the Hispanic and general US population who believed that jobs were difficult to find where they lived – 78 per cent versus 73 per cent. Likewise, not surprisingly, Hispanics were found more likely than the general population to rate their personal situation as poor or fair – 75 per cent as against 61 per cent. Also, more than 84 per cent of foreign-born Hispanics reported that their finances were in either poor or fair shape, compared to 66 per cent of US-born Hispanics (Lopez et al., 2009).

In all OECD countries, the unemployment rate for the foreign-born increased markedly between the first three quarters of 2008 and 2009, generally exceeding the rate for nationals. In the EU-15 member states, for example, the increase, on average, was 3.4 per cent, twice the rate for nationals, according to the OECD (2010a).

During an economic crisis, declining labour demand often obliges workers to accept part-time jobs although they want to work full time. Due to their higher vulnerability to joblessness, migrants are more likely to be driven to this situation than non-migrants. The differentiated impact on employment for migrants and non-migrants can also be seen by comparing their respective shares in part-time employment. During 2008–2009, the number of foreign-born persons in part-time employment increased sharply, and the figure was higher than that for nationals in a number of OECD countries. If these part-time jobs (reflecting underemployment) were excluded, this would push up the unemployment rates for migrants and increase the gap between the unemployment rates for the two groups.

In Spain, the unemployment rate for immigrants was roughly 50 per cent higher than that for all Spanish workers in 2008. When general unemployment was at 11.3 per cent, the rate was 17.5 per cent for foreigners. Other reports suggest that migrants lost jobs at twice the rate for Spaniards (Duran, 2008; *Financial Times*, 2009i). The overall unemployment rate in Ireland stood at 7 per cent between June and August 2008; the rate of unemployment for Irish nationals was 6.6 per cent, compared with 9 per cent for non-Irish nationals (Central Statistics Office Ireland, 2008). In

France, for a male migrant worker from Algeria who arrived in 2001 or later, the relative risk of being unemployed was 11 times higher than that for a French national (IILS, 2010).[31]

Other vulnerable domestic groups, including internal migrants, could be exposed to similar discrimination. For example, in China, established local residents were favoured over internal migrant workers in state redevelopment and compensation schemes. To illustrate, in 2008, the municipal government kick-started the redevelopment of Sunhe and Cuigezhuang, areas that were attractive to big property developers. In May 2008, under a model which it hoped to apply to hundreds of other villages, the government resettled near Beijing close to 2,000 families from a village in the Cuigezhuang area. The resident farmers were given modern apartments free of charge. The migrant workers who lived alongside their farmer landlords in the village for years were left out of the compensation deals (*Financial Times*, 2009ai).

How recession also constrains the upward mobility of migrants and sharpens inequality

A similar disharmony is often found in the earnings of migrants and non-migrants. As in the case of employment, when the economy is on an upward swing and immigrants become increasingly integrated into the labour market, their wages over time tend to catch up with those of domestic workers, helping them to achieve upward labour mobility. The danger of discrimination tends to decline. However, in times of economic downturn, the process slows down or simply does not work. These fluctuations in wages are generally sharper for migrants than for non-migrants.

For example, in the United States, the incomes of non-citizen households were 4.1 per cent higher in 2006 than in 2005, but the incomes of all US households had increased only by 0.7 per cent. However, by 2007, the median annual income of non-citizens – a group that accounted for 7 per cent of all US households and 52 per cent of all immigrant households – had already fallen by 7.3 per cent, while the median annual income of all US households increased by 1.3 per cent during the same period (Kochhar, 2008c). In the construction industry, which had a heavy concentration of Hispanic workers, weekly earnings for most groups slipped in the first quarter of 2008, compared with the same period in 2007, but foreign-born Hispanics were worse off. Day labourers who used to earn about USD 10 an hour felt lucky to have jobs at the rate of USD 7 or USD 8 per hour (*Financial Times*, 2009ab).

[31] IILS estimates based on national labour force surveys (1996–2009).

In Spain, the gap between the earnings of Spanish nationals and African migrants was striking; it increased with age and, for each age group, somewhat surprisingly, with education. For instance, African migrant workers aged 16–34 years with a primary education earned 10 per cent less than their Spanish counterparts, but the gap increased to more than 50 per cent for the university-educated, aged 35–59 years (IILS, 2010).[32]

In the United States, the general feeling of inequality may also be rising because of the: (a) stagnation in wage growth relative to several other types of incomes and (b) the tension between those who can hold on to their jobs and those who are finding it hard to find any work. Recessions normally slow down wage growth. In the mid-1970s economic downturn, real weekly pay fell by 7 per cent, and in the 1980s recession, it declined by 4 per cent. However, during the most recent (2008–2009) recession, the situation looked somewhat different. Although some companies cut wages, the average hourly wage rate rose 1.5 per cent to 2.5 per cent during 2008–2009. The actual rise in pay was slightly less due to cuts in working hours, but a typical worker nonetheless received a 1–2 per cent inflation-adjusted raise over the year, according to a US Department of Labor report. In January 2010, the Department of Labor reported a rise of 0.5 per cent in wages and benefits in the three months ending December 2009 and a rise of 1.5 per cent for the whole year. Though this wage and benefits hike was better than in other deep recessions, it was the weakest since 1982. As mentioned in chapter 1, there was a decline in the median middle-class income as well.

If this was fomenting a feeling of resentment among working men and women, those without work, particularly migrants and other disadvantaged groups, were paying a still heavier price, because new hiring plummeted and finding a new job became extremely difficult for them. In the United States, soaring inequality and stagnant real income have long been features of the national economy. In a study, Raghuram Rajan of the University of Chicago noted that "of every dollar of real income growth that was generated over 31 years between 1976 and 2007, 58 cents went to the top 1 per cent of the households" (Rajan, 2010). The crisis seems to be making the situation worse.

Data collected by Sir Tony Atkinson of Nuffield College and his colleagues at Harvard University showed that recessions tended to increase income inequality. Evidence showed that following the Nordic banking crises of the 1990s, income inequality increased in these countries, as the richest

[32] IILS estimates based on national labour force surveys (1996–2009).

1 per cent of the population received rising shares of income. Similar trends were discernible in Spain in the 1980s and in Japan in the 1990s. An exception was the Great Depression of the 1930s in the United States, when bank failures and loss of savings led to a huge fall in the share of income held by the rich. The discussion in chapter 1 has also shown that in the United States, the economic costs of recession-driven joblessness were being disproportionately borne by those who were already poor.[33]

If the current differentiated trends in jobs and wages take hold or worsen, the glaring inequality that has become a disquieting development in most countries would be further aggravated. This could easily generate popular anger and resentment and sow the seeds of social tension. As noted, migrants are often among the worst victims of rising inequality, especially in times of economic crisis. And yet, there is a potential danger that popular anger and resentment over inequality and deprivation could turn against migrants in the form of a rising wave of anti-immigrant feeling.

An increase in irregular migration, abuse of human and labour rights and erosion of respect for the law go hand-in hand

When job-related visa-holding migrants lose their jobs and decide to go underground, thus swelling the informal sector in the host country, and new inflows of irregular migrants join them, there is a real danger that migrants would become victims of exploitation and human rights abuse that goes beyond discrimination in the workplace. If this happens on a large scale, it could lead to an erosion of respect for law and ethical values, including a more generalized degeneration of social and human rights conditions in the host country. In such a climate, there could even be violence against migrants, and this might eventually extend to other vulnerable groups as well. During the Asian financial crisis, although the impact on migrant stocks was limited, there was tense competition between local and foreign workers in a shrinking labour market, with rising xenophobia in countries such as Indonesia, where an estimated 100,000 ethnic Chinese left for neighbouring countries.

There were already some incipient, but nonetheless alarming, signs that in the absence of vigilance, such situations could develop at least in some countries during the current crisis as well. As a United Nations Development Programme (UNDP) report noted, the governments of some destination countries have stepped up the enforcement of migration laws in ways that could infringe on the rights of migrants. In Russia, industrial unrest such as auto-workers strikes against dismissals and rising resentment against unemployment and wage

[33] Some economists also believe that income inequality could help create asset price bubbles and contribute to financial fragility and economic crisis.

cuts coincided with growing violence against jobless immigrants by racist skinheads. The Sova Centre, a Moscow–based organization that monitors hate crimes, estimated that there were 428 racially motivated attacks in Russia in 2008 that left 97 people dead; it cautioned that the actual situation might be even worse than these figures suggest (*Financial Times*, 2009g). In Italy, there were reports of attacks on Romanian workers in Rome. Amid a tense social climate, Roma Gypsies, already a vulnerable and disadvantaged group, became scapegoats for lack of jobs and increasing crime in Hungary.

Economic insecurity and increasing anti-immigrant feeling, alongside rising irregular migration, make migrant integration more difficult

Integration of migration is one of the most challenging aspects of migration management. A number of countries, including France, Germany, Italy and the Netherlands, had already been facing difficulties dealing with it. The recession added to these difficulties. In a climate of rising economic insecurity and shrinking jobs and other opportunities, populist slogans that seek to make migrants scapegoats for joblessness, rising social security costs and other economic and social ills often gain ground. Once this happens and extreme political parties try to cash in on these slogans, fomenting anti-immigrant feeling, integration difficulties would certainly be exacerbated in receiving countries. A survey by the Pew Research Center in spring 2007 revealed that even before the recession, more than 40 per cent of the people in Italy, the UK, France, Germany and Spain had a negative perception of the impact of immigration in their countries (see Figure 7). It is quite likely that since then the increasing pressure on jobs and earnings and a tense environment of economic uncertainty caused by the recession have made the situation worse.

Figure 7: Those who say immigration has a negative influence (%)

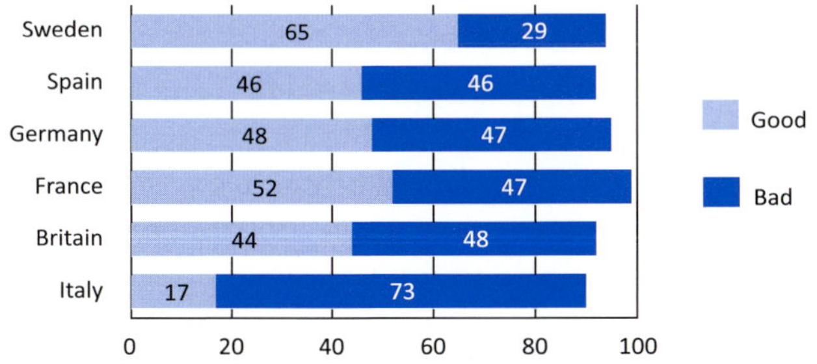

Source: Menasce Horowitz, 2010.

Another source of integration difficulties linked to the recession was the likely increase in irregular migration and the expansion of the underground economy. Fearful of detection, irregular migrants would shy away from integration programmes. In an atmosphere of fear and suspicion, confidence-building between immigrants and the receiving society – a critical element in successful integration – would be more difficult.

An increase in new immigration flows of non-working-age migrants and those with low labour market outcome poses a serious challenge to migration integration and management

As discussed in chapter 2, in a number of rich countries, recent inflows are set to show a relative increase in the number of non-working-age migrants (i.e. persons too young or too old to work) and those who, though of working age, have a low labour market outcome due to their entry through non-labour migration (e.g. family reunification and humanitarian) channels. An increase in the number of non-working-age persons entails additional economic and social costs for the receiving country, but without the benefits that working migrants normally bring to the economy. When underage migrants subsequently join the labour force in these countries, they could be a bonus to the ageing society, provided however that they are adequately trained and effectively employed. It is worth noting that the working-age population in OECD countries is expected to increase by only 1.9 per cent in the next 10 years, compared with an increase of 8.6 per cent between 2000 and 2010 (OECD, 2010a).[34] In the EU, the working-age population will shrink by 20 million between 2005 and 2050, and the number of those over 65 years will increase by 40 million.

However, if these young migrants do not gain access to educational and job opportunities and remain unemployed and disgruntled, they could be a worrisome source of social unrest. The fact that the same receiving countries already have a high rate of youth unemployment and that this portends to continue in the coming years only add to the seriousness of the problem.

The relative increase in the entry of working-age migrants through humanitarian channels poses a similar challenge to a certain extent, because of the generally low employment outcome for these migrants. In the absence of proactive measures to enhance the integration of such migrants into the labour market, they may not be able to make a full contribution to the economy of the host country and instead add to the economic strain (see, in this connection, the discussion in chapter 5).

[34] In connection with this discussion, see chapter 5 on likely future changes in demographic trends.

3.2 Effects on home countries

Declining outflows can increase pressure on unemployment in labour-abundant countries

The recession, as discussed in chapter 2, has slowed down new migration flows. However, it is too early to make precise estimates of how long this trend would persist and what might be the magnitude of the decline, if any, in migration flows in the coming years. If, however, the trend continues, as had happened in the 1920s and 1930s, it would have some important effects on migrant-sending countries.

How will such a decline affect the unemployment situation in labour-abundant countries? Although reduced unemployment in the sending country is generally considered to be one of the positive contributions of migration, its potential in doing so should not be overrated. There are several reasons for this. First, barring a few exceptions, emigration normally does not involve more than 3–4 per cent of the domestic labour force – too small to make a dent in widespread unemployment. Even a much higher level of emigration may prove relatively ineffective when the problem is structural and demographic pressures continue to be strong – as reflected in the experiences of a number of countries, including Mexico, the Philippines, Sri Lanka and Turkey.[35] Further, excessive reliance on emigration as a relief to unemployment could encourage the sending country to postpone unpopular but essential economic reform, as had happened in several eastern Mediterranean countries in the 1960s and early 1970s. Over time, this could only aggravate the unemployment situation and undermine long-term growth (see also the section on remittances).

Even so, there is little doubt that labour migration can provide some temporary relief from unemployment, especially in overcrowded areas. In addition, when other conditions are favourable, labour migration can help a country absorb an *increase* in the labour force, as it did, for example, in countries such as Pakistan, the Republic of Korea and Sri Lanka at different periods in time. Experience also shows that circular migration can reduce fluctuations in employment levels. No less important, in periods of economic transition and falling living standards, labour outflows can serve as a safety valve against mass discontent, as was witnessed in Central and Eastern Europe in the wake of the fall of the Berlin Wall in 1989.

[35] For a more detailed discussion on the effects of migration in sending countries, see Ghosh (1996, 1997).

Further, labour migration could be helpful in reducing fiscal pressure resulting from unemployment-related welfare programmes. In Egypt, the employment guarantee scheme may not have worked in the 1970s without the massive emigration of its workers to the Gulf States (World Bank, 1995). Not surprisingly, in the past, a number of widely diverse developing countries, such as Bangladesh, Barbados, the Dominican Republic, El Salvador, Guatemala, India, Morocco, Pakistan, the Philippines, Tunisia, Turkey and Viet Nam, encouraged labour emigration for several reasons: labour emigration was envisioned to relieve pressure on unemployment and was seen as a source of external financial resources, among others (this is further discussed in the section on remittances).

Although, as mentioned above, labour outflows may not be an effective answer to widespread, structural unemployment in developing countries, it cannot be denied that if the recession-related trend towards falling migration were to take hold, this would make the unemployment situation even more difficult for a number of small countries, especially those that have less diversified and less flexible economies and rely on the employment abroad of large numbers of people relative to their workforce. This would include countries with overcrowded local areas that have been benefiting from high emigration to cope with employment pressure.

As labour outflows from low-wage countries to high-wage countries and total demand for labour increase, this could, in principle, raise wages in the origin country. Does this mean that a slowdown in migration would have a negative effect on wages in sending countries? It does not seem very likely. While it is true that mass migration in the nineteenth and early twentieth century from poorer countries in Europe (e.g. Sweden and Ireland) to richer European countries led to a rise in wages and narrowed intercountry inequality (Williamson, 2002), things are no longer exactly the same.

Given the size of the unused labour reserve due to unemployment and underemployment in most developing countries, emigration hardly pushes up wages at the macro level, although large-scale migration can cause temporary labour shortages in specific sectors or local areas, leading to a rise in wages. This happened, for example, in Yemen between 1975 and 1977, in Pakistan in the late 1970s, and in the Republic of Korea between 1975 and 1980. The converse is also true. Therefore, it is not at all sure that a fall in migration flows, except in the unlikely event of a dramatic decline following the recession, would have any generalized effect on wages in migrant-sending developing countries, although it may add to an already difficult unemployment situation.

Does the loss of skilled personnel in rich countries imply equal gains for poor countries?

The discussion in chapter 2 has shown that, due to the recession, a number of migrant-receiving countries have become less enthusiastic even about skilled immigrants and that some skilled migrants might return home. To what extent should these "brain gains" help developing countries? Even though, as discussed above, the loss of skilled workers might harm the growth and competitiveness of industrial countries, should the potential gains in skills make much difference for origin countries in the developing world?

Losses of skills are generally considered to be harmful for developing countries. However, in making a judicious assessment of the real situation, several considerations must be taken into account. First, for developing countries to reap immediate gains from return or retention (non-emigration) of skills as a result of the recession, skills need to be fully attuned to the technological or economic needs of these countries. This, however, is not always the case, nor is it sure that the conditions that inhibit the effective utilization of available skills in these countries would necessarily change within a short span of time.

Experience in several countries/areas, including Taiwan Province of China and India, shows that when return of skilled personnel is voluntary and properly planned in advance and macroeconomic conditions, including the business environment, in origin countries are favourable, this could be a powerful driving force for growth, especially in specific sectors (Ghosh, ed., 2000a). However, sudden or imposed return as a result of a crisis in the host country is not likely to meet these preconditions.

Second, some theoretical and empirical studies have suggested that, depending on the levels of adult education and rates of emigration of persons with tertiary education, some countries (e.g. Brazil and China) can actually benefit from skilled migration, while some other countries or areas (e.g. El Salvador, Guyana, Jamaica, and Trinidad and Tobago) may find this harmful (Beine et al., 2001; Lowell, 2004). Under this "optimal skilled migration models", much depends on the country-specific situation, especially the proportion of a country's skilled migrants abroad to the total number of its skilled workers and the quality and structure of its education system. This apart, it is widely recognized that for countries with a broad and flexible base of human resources and the capacity to easily replace outflows, skill migration is not a major problem. A sample-based analysis by Beine et al. (2001) showed that although more countries would lose than gain from skilled migration, the winners would include the most populous states that represent 80 per cent of the sample. The authors also found that, except for countries like Jamaica and Guyana with very high emigration rates, the net variation of losses (or gains) in terms of GDP growth rates per capita was less than 0.20 per cent per year.

Third, and equally important, skilled migration need not be seen as a permanent loss for the sending country. Recent global changes, including market integration and progress in information and communication systems, make it possible for the origin country to establish transnational links with its diasporas and tap their skills, talents and other resources. This happens when ethnic networking leads scientists and technicians at home to establish close personal contacts with those of the same national origin who are now living and working abroad in a technologically advanced country. This has already started happening. A paper by Agrawal et al. (2008) lends support to this view. It found that Indian scientists who work in India but seek patents in the United States draw heavily on the work of scientists of Indian origin in the United States, even if very similar research is also done by others with whom they do not have ethnic ties. Thus, if the transnational links of a scientific diaspora community are properly utilized (an important precondition), it can yield benefits all around – for the host country, the immigrant scientists and the home country, its scientists and its economy. There is also the libertarian argument of individual freedom of movement and the right to place one's talent in the world market.

These general caveats notwithstanding, a slowdown of skilled migration could actually be beneficial for some countries or in certain situations. When poor countries that are short of human capital lose many of their most talented workers, this can be a major impediment to future growth and technological progress. As past experiences in several countries in sub-Saharan Africa, Latin America and the Caribbean have shown, the initial cost of skill migration could be compounded by a second round of negative effects that undermine the training of intermediary cadres and inhibit product and process innovation. In addition, since human skills often complement capital and technology, skilled migration could depress the wages of unskilled workers and lower the average income of the non-migrant population (Ghosh, 1997). Also, to the extent that public funds are used to support education, skilled migration implies loss of public investment in human capital. Skilled migration boosts the tax revenues of receiving countries, but depletes them in sending countries. A study by Harvard University showed that 1 million Indians living in the United States accounted for 0.1 per cent of India's population, but they earned the equivalent of 10 per cent of India's national income (Desai et al., 2001). In India, these Indians would have earned less, but they probably would have been among the highest taxpayers. The 50 million people who live outside mainland China (including Taiwan Province of China) earned an annual income equivalent to two thirds of China's GDP in 2001 (Devan and Tewari, 2001).

The snag in this line of argument is that a country's fiscal loss from migration can be more than offset by remittances, as has recently been the case in India (although the nature of the impact of the two on the economy may not be exactly the same). Goldfarb et al. (1984) used a model to analyse the economic impact of Filipino physicians moving to the United States. Their findings, based on a set of reasonable assumptions, were that those who remained in the Philippines would benefit. Second and more important, in many sending countries, available skills, in any case, remain idle or are not effectively utilized, leading to a huge waste of human capital – a situation characterized by some analysts as "brain in the drain". This is because of the mismatch between the educational curricula and system and the real skill needs of the economy and various other constraints.

Even so, in several of the cases mentioned above, a slowdown in skilled emigration or the restoration of such skills through return would be useful, provided that these skills are effectively utilized. From this perspective, it is understandable why African, Caribbean and Pacific countries expressed concern that the recent EU proposal for issuing "Blue Card" visas for skilled personnel from third-country (non-EU) nationals could be harmful for Africa, although much depends on the country-specific situation. There is some evidence that the recession has accelerated the return of skilled migrants to African countries such as Nigeria, Ghana, Kenya and Angola. These migrants are anxious to play an entrepreneurial or managerial role in some of the new or dynamic sectors of their home economies. However, many of them would also like to maintain their transnational links and keep doors open in their erstwhile host countries. This obviously calls for reciprocal arrangements to facilitate mobility between countries.

Even countries with a relatively solid human capital base can benefit if returning skills meet changing needs and shortages in specific sectors. India, for instance, plans to spend USD 100 billion over the next few years on much-needed infrastructure, but it faces a shortfall of more than half the skilled human resources required to modernize its infrastructure over the next 10 years, according to a World Bank study. One reason for this is that more graduates are attracted by better-paid jobs in the IT sector, for example, or by jobs abroad. India could possibly gain from the return of some of its civil engineers if they can be steered to and effectively used in the infrastructure-sector modernization programme.

How will the return of migrants affect home countries?

There remains the question of return flows. Mass expulsions similar to what happened in Nigeria in 1983 and in Ghana in 1969, or large-scale returns, as was witnessed during the 1990–1991 Gulf War, could seriously dislocate the economies of origin countries. The unexpected repatriation of 1.5 million Egyptian workers and their dependents during the Gulf Crisis threw the country's budget out of gear, just as the sudden return of large numbers of Indian migrant workers put the economy of the Indian state of Kerala under heavy strain. Jordan and Yemen faced similar difficulties when their migrant workers were forced to return. During the Asian financial crisis, the Indonesian economy badly suffered as a result of the return of its migrant workers. During the Great Depression of the 1930s, the return of Mexicans and Europeans from the United States surely did not help matters in countries of origin.

There is, however, no indication that the present economic crisis would trigger any mass expulsion (which is unlawful under international law) or massive return as was witnessed during past economic or political upheavals. As already mentioned, in Poland, the massive return of migrants anticipated by the government in 2007 did not materialize.

This is not to suggest that the impact of large-scale return flows on home countries is not of any importance. The discussion in chapter 2 has shown that the recession has increased migrants' return, though not in the form of massive human waves. Aside from its likely negative impact on remittance flows (discussed in the next section), the unexpected return of large numbers of migrants will no doubt place additional strain on the job market, as well as on the social and physical infrastructure of sending countries, especially those poor countries that have traditionally relied on high emigration as a mainstay of their economies with relatively low levels of return. Intense, often fierce, competition over jobs and limited social services and amenities in the wake of large-scale return could easily add to social tension and conflict in these countries.

Economic woes and threats to livelihood could lead to a rise in irregular migration and human trafficking

If the crisis continues and economic woes worsen in poor countries, the situation can build pressure for irregular migration and encourage human trafficking. Driven by poverty and despair, many in these countries could be impelled to seek escape abroad and, in the absence of opportunities for legal admission, they could try to enter by irregular channels. This, in turn, could encourage human trafficking. Elsewhere, based on empirical evidence, I have argued that the poor surely travel to neighbouring countries, but not infrequently to distant lands as well (Ghosh, 1997, 1998). If sufficient funds cannot be raised, for example, by selling modest family possessions or by borrowing, all that a future migrant has to do is sign a bond with a trafficker or an agent for deferred payment for which the migrant and the family at home may assume responsibility. The trafficker would generally welcome this, as the bond symbolizes a migrant's servitude for many years to come, if not forever. For the trafficker, the bond would open the gates for abuse and exploitation of the victim; even the family at home may not be spared.

Despite the tightening of both national and international laws against migrant smuggling and human trafficking, the danger seems quite real in the situation created by the economic crisis. It should not be forgotten that, in times of economic difficulty, employers in the destination country, especially marginal firms and those operating in the black economy, tend to collude with traffickers in order to benefit from irregular, and therefore cheap and docile, labour. This increases the danger.

It is widely known that getting to the destination country by irregular channels often entails not only life-threatening dangers, but also exposure to exploitation, extortion and human rights abuse. The recent recession seems to have aggravated some of these problems. For instance, according to human rights associations that monitor migration to the United States across Mexican borders, organized crime groups have begun taking aim at migrants from Mexico as well as those from Central and South America as major sources of illicit revenue. They use kidnapping, physical violence and even murder as their means of action.

Non-Mexicans were more vulnerable, given that they were less familiar with their surroundings and less likely to report to the authorities (*The New York Times*, 2009g).

3.3 Remittance flows: Rewards and risks

How big is the likely decline in future remittance flows? Why is assessment so difficult?

As briefly noted in chapter 2, migrants' remittances to developing countries rose sharply in recent years (see Table 3). In 2008, remittances totalled USD 338 billion, which was more than twice the amount received by developing countries as recently as 2002. Not surprisingly, in the wake of the economic crisis, falling new migration flows and increasing return, migrants' joblessness and lower earnings in host countries, combined with their growing feeling of uncertainty, have continued to put downward pressure on remittance flows.

In November 2008, the World Bank, which follows remittance trends carefully, estimated a likely fall of 0.9 per cent for 2009 (or, in a worst-case scenario, a decline of no more than 6%).[36] As the global economic situation was then rapidly worsening, I had argued that the lower end of the remittance decline envisaged by the World Bank for 2009 in November 2008 was most probably an underestimate. Since then and up to the time of writing, the World Bank, in keeping with the revised rates of global economic growth, has systematically updated its forecasts on future remittance flows: in March 2009, it expected remittances for 2009 to fall by 5–8 per cent; three months later, it further raised the anticipated rate of decline to 7–10 per cent. In November 2009, the World Bank again revised these figures, suggesting a decline of 6.1 per cent for 2009 and a small increase of 1.4 per cent for 2010.

Table 3: Outlook for remittance flows to developing countries, 2009–2011

USD billion	***2006***	***2007***	***2008***	***2009e***	***2010f***	***2011f***
Developing countries	**235**	**289**	**338**	**317**	**322**	**334**
East Asia and Pacific	58	71	86	85	85	89
Europe and Central Asia	37	51	58	49	51	53
Latin America and Caribbean	59	63	65	58	59	61
Middle East and North Africa	26	31	35	32	33	34
South Asia	43	54	73	72	73	76
Sub-Saharan Africa	13	19	21	21	21	22
Low-income countries	20	25	32	32	33	34
Middle-income countries	215	265	306	285	289	300
World	317	385	444	420	425	441
Growth rate (%)						
Developing countries	**18.3%**	**22.9%**	**16.7%**	**-6.1%**	**1.4%**	**3.9%**
East Asia and Pacific	14.1%	23.8%	20.8%	-1.5%	0.8%	3.7%
Europe and Central Asia	24.1%	36.0%	13.8%	-14.7%	2.7%	5.0%
Latin America and Caribbean	18.1%	6.8%	2.3%	-9.6%	0.5%	3.5%
Middle East and North Africa	4.6%	20.1%	10.6%	-7.2%	1.5%	3.3%
South Asia	25.3%	27.1%	35.6%	-1.8%	1.7%	4.1%
Sub-Saharan Africa	34.7%	47.6%	13.4%	-2.9%	1.8%	3.9%
Low-income countries	23.9%	23.4%	28.3%	0.7%	2.6%	4.6%
Middle-income countries	17.8%	22.9%	15.6%	-6.8%	1.2%	3.8%
World	15.3%	21.3%	15.3%	-5.3%	1.2%	3.7%

Source: World Bank, 2009a.

The determinants of remittance behaviour and flows are complex and volatile. This makes it difficult to work out dependable forecasts of remittance flows.

[36] Total remittances to developing countries for 2008 were then estimated at USD 283 billion, instead of USD 338 billion, as revised in November 2009.

The well-known fact that a large proportion of total remittances (50% or more) is transferred through unofficial channels is not the only problem. The different determinants or variables that influence remittance flows cannot be easily captured or fed into a workable model to make remittance forecasts for future years. The World Bank uses the share of remittance outflows in the GDP of host countries worldwide as a basis for preparing its remittance forecasts. As the GDP of host countries goes down during an economic crisis such as the present one, so does the total amount of remittances (being a share of the GDP) and vice versa.

The World Bank does well in taking due account of the effects of changes in the GDP of host countries on remittance flows, but it recognizes that several other important determinants, such as the cost of transaction, are left out owing to the difficulty of modelling these elements. More importantly, it assumes that the share of remittances in the GDP of host countries would remain constant. However, the dynamics of the situation clearly suggest that both these variables (not just the GDP but also the share of remittances in GDP) and, consequently, the ratio between them are likely to change during the economic crisis. Aside from possible deaths among older migrants, some depletion, or least a deceleration in growth, of the migrant stock may be caused by a higher rate of return of existing migrants alongside a falling rate of new immigration, as discussed in chapter 2 (the World Bank does consider this but only in examining the low-case scenario). Any depletion of the migrant stock (including new arrivals) should have a depressive effect on the level of remittances as well. Further, it is well known that, compared to recent migrants, settled migrants (including those who have become naturalized citizens of the destination country) tend to remit less as family links in the home country tend to weaken over time, with the possible exception of cases where remittances are primarily investment-oriented.

Even if it is assumed that the migrant stock would remain the same, their remittances could fall at a higher rate than the national income for several reasons. Fist, as discussed in chapter 3, during the recent recession, the decline in several sectors with high concentrations of migrants may have been sharper than for the economy as a whole. Also, as earlier discussion has shown, in times of recession, migrants generally lose more than the non-migrants in terms of both jobs and wages; in other words, the income inequality between migrants and non-migrants increases. It would be logical therefore to assume that the rate of decline in migrants' income and remittances would be higher than the overall rate of GDP decline.

Further, it is not just the number of migrants but also their composition and characteristics that matter. As discussed in chapter 2, recent flows to a number of OECD countries showed a relative increase in the share of non-working-age migrants and persons who entered through humanitarian (as distinct from labour migration) channels. Clearly, in general, persons who are too young or too old to work cannot be expected to have earnings of their own. Also, since they enter mostly through the family reunification channel, their living expenses will be an additional charge on the income of existing migrants. They would thus have less money available to send home and also much less need to do so. As for humanitarian migrants of working age, it is well known that they have a low labour market (employment) outcome. Consequently, on average, they would earn less and probably remit less than labour migrants.[37] This makes it important to also take due account of the labour market participation rates of migrants and other related characteristics – and not just the number of migrants – in projecting future remittance flows.

Finally, there is the important question of the propensity of migrants to remit as distinct from their (earnings-based) capacity to send money home. Extreme uncertainty about the economy of the host country and the migrants' own future has been found to lead many migrants to be more cautious and send less money home than in normal times. Exceptionally and for a short while, migrants may cut back on their own consumption to maintain the same level of remittances sent to their families back home, as some migrants in Dubai may have done.[38] However, this has its limits. In case of a sharp deterioration of their economic situation and prolonged uncertainty about their future, most migrants are also more likely to economize on remittances. Not surprisingly, more than one in seven of Mexican immigrants to the United States who had sent money home in the previous two years remitted less in 2008. For 80 per cent of these Mexican immigrants, the main reason was economic decline and uncertainty. In 2008, less than 8 per cent of Latino immigrants sent lower amounts than in the previous year, but the percentage rose to nearly 45 per cent in 2009 (see Figure 8) (Lopez et al., 2009).

Further, it should not be forgotten that, in many cases, even family budget-oriented remittances include a component that covers home improvements and other small investments, as well as discretionary social events and religious festivities. When times are really bad in both host and home countries, migrants are likely to economize on remittances by postponing expenses on some of these items. In most cases, the same would apply to collective remittances that in normal times might be spent on projects for promoting community welfare. The more remittances assume the role of investment capital, the more sensitive they are likely to be to

[37] However, there may be situations where refugees in the host country may be able to raise funds from local sources and send money home to help other victims of persecution who had been left behind, including for their escape abroad.

[38] Information based on interviews reported in Ratha et al. (2009b).

the economic downturn. This also explains why the counter-cyclic role of remittances in home countries does not work when both home and host countries face serious economic meltdown and migrants are fearful of their own future.

Figure 8: Remittances from Latino immigrants

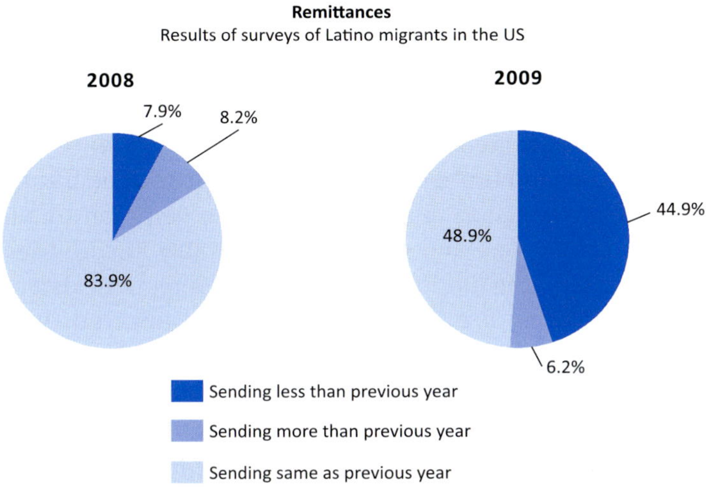

Source: Lopez et al., 2009.

These caveats notwithstanding, the World Bank forecasts served well to signal the likely decline in remittances in 2009, even when the fact that returning migrants were most likely to send their savings home was taken into account. It should be noted that when returnees do so, they are likely to take at least part of the savings with them in cash or in kind (reducing money transfer though formal financial channels).[39] On the other hand, it is possible that fears about increasing anti-terrorist restrictions on money transfers may lead some migrants to temporarily increase their remittances, as had happened, for example, in Pakistan in 2001–2002.

Overall, according to the World Bank, there could be a slight increase in remittances in 2010, but the increase would be much smaller than that in 2007. In the worst-case scenario, the decline would actually continue through 2010, although the scale of decline would be quite small (see Table 3).

While remittances to all developing countries were estimated to show a relative decline in 2009, the extent of the decline, according to a World Bank

[39] In the case of the Philippines, for example, Rodriguez (1996) noted that "regular cash transfers account for about 26 per cent of total transfers; most of the rest is cash brought home on return." Some put the figure as high as 35 per cent (or 42%, including in-kind transfers), according to Puri and Ritzema (1999).

estimate, varied from one region to another. Eastern Europe and Central Asia saw the steepest declines, followed by Latin America and the Caribbean. Remittance flows to the latter region until the third quarter showed larger declines than the World Bank had forecasted earlier. The decline for South Asia, as well as for East Asia and the Pacific, was more moderate, and remittance flows to these two regions proved stronger than had been expected earlier.

The differentiated rates of decline in different regions were largely influenced by related conditions, including policy trends in host regions that affected migrant flows and stocks. Rates of decline may also have been influenced by differences in the composition and labour market characteristics of migrants. However, some of the basic recession-related factors were common to all. The sharp decline in Eastern Europe and Central Asia, notably in countries such as Tajikistan, Kyrgyzstan, the Republic of Moldova and Uzbekistan, were largely due to deteriorating economic conditions that affected their migrants and the decline in new migration inflows to the Russian Federation and Kazakhstan. The sharp depreciation of the Russian rouble against the US dollar, alongside falling oil prices, accelerated the decline in dollar terms. If the oil price continues to rise again, the situation could gradually change. The decline in remittances to sub-Saharan Africa was largely due to the negative effects of the recession on jobs and wages and on migration flows in host countries both within Africa and outside the continent, notably the EU and the United States.

As for Latin America and the Caribbean, a decline in employment and wages (which had a more severe effect on Hispanic migrants than the general population) in the construction and manufacturing industries, a drop in the cash savings of migrants, lower new immigration, and an increase in deportation, partly from worksite raids, were among the main causes of the decline in remittances.[40] Although remittances to South Asia were relatively stable, the biggest concern was the slowdown in oil-producing Gulf Cooperation Council (GCC) countries, which accounted for 40 per cent of total remittance flows to South Asia and for 60 per cent of flows to Bangladesh and Sri Lanka.

[40] It is worth noting that the Inter-American Development Bank foresaw a sharper decline in remittances from Latin America than the World Bank did. The projected fall of remittances from the United States to Latin America, according to the IADB, would be of the order of 11 per cent in 2009. The Bank of Mexico estimated that remittances from the United States for the first 11 months of 2009 declined by 16 per cent compared to the same period in the previous year.

Why are remittances important for developing countries? Can they spur development?[41]

The positive role that remittances play in developing countries is now well documented. By contributing directly to the family budget, including expenditures on food and housing as well as health and hygiene, remittances not only promote family welfare and improve living standards, but also help develop future human capital. In a number of countries, including Bangladesh, Senegal and Turkey, remittances accounted for a high proportion of the household income of recipient families. They were used to meet expenses for basic needs, although sometimes they also encouraged conspicuous consumption amidst a preference for imported luxury goods. In Latin America and the Caribbean, remittances were estimated to support more than 50 million people.

Evidence from a number of diverse countries, including El Salvador, Jordan, Mexico, the Philippines and Thailand, suggests that remittances raised school attendance and the level of children's education and helped reduce child slavery. A continuing fall in the inflow of remittances would weaken its positive role in all these areas.

However, remittances are not spent only on household consumption; they often also contribute to the upgrading of farm production and the growth of income-generating small businesses in local areas, and thus increase family income while promoting local development. By removing credit constraints and providing risk insurance, remittances encourage the use of improved technology and production inputs, leading to output growth, as was found in several Asian countries, including Pakistan and Thailand. Although in the Caribbean and Pacific islands as well as in Morocco, emigration and remittances were initially associated with a decline in farm production, experience in sub-Saharan Africa and Asia, including China, showed that the situation changes over time and often leads to farm modernization and increased crop production.

A steady stream of remittances also helps the development of small enterprises in the non-farm sector and promotes entrepreneurial skills, although sometimes, in the absence of proper guidance and timely assistance, remittance-backed small enterprises have been found to fail. Evidence across countries and regions shows that collective remittances can make a significant contribution to local development, since they help build social assets and facilities such as schools, hospitals, community centres, feeder roads and various small infrastructure projects.

[41] For a fuller discussion of the issues raised in this and the following two sections, see Ghosh (2006).

While the positive contributions of remittances both at the household and local levels are well recognized, there is no clear evidence that remittances by themselves can spur sustainable development at the macro or national level. For this to happen, conditions need to be created to prime the economy for development. A major constraining factor is the lack of adequate product and credit market integration, which seriously circumscribes the transmission of local-level growth impulses created by the multiplier effect of remittances to other parts of the national economy. It also increases the risk of building inflationary pressure due to supply constraints in remittance-receiving towns and villages.

Even so, remittances, which are larger than export earnings in a number of small developing countries, could provide valuable support to the balance of payments and help development through imports of essential inputs. Remittances may not be a propelling force for trade policy reform or economic openness, but countries may find them helpful – as India did in the 1990s – in tiding over temporary foreign exchange difficulties following trade liberalization. In recent years, several countries, including Brazil, El Salvador, Mexico, Panama and Turkey, successfully used remittances as collateral to raise funds in the international capital market. As mentioned in chapter 1, just before the present economic crisis, several African governments were set to launch similar securitization-of-remittances schemes to raise funds at a lower cost than borrowing on sovereign credit, but they had to postpone action due to the impact of the crisis on the international capital market.

Remittances have a significant potential to alleviate poverty

Household surveys and other studies have revealed the links between remittances and poverty alleviation, although the degree of causality is less clear. A cross-country IMF study showed that, on average, a 25-percentage-point increase in the remittances/GDP ratio was associated with less than a 0.5-percentage-point decrease in the share of people living in poverty (Spatafora, 2005). Another study based on data from 71 developing countries suggested that, depending on the variables used, a 10 per cent increase in the share of migrants in a country's population would lead to a decline of between 2.1 per cent and 3 per cent in the share of those living on less than USD 1 a day (Adams and Page, 2005). There is little doubt about the impact of remittances on alleviating the hardships of poverty when a high proportion of family remittances is spent on food and other basic necessities of life. This indeed was the case in countries such as El Salvador, Guatemala and Nicaragua, as well as Bangladesh, Senegal and Turkey, as already mentioned.

However, much seems to depend on who migrates: with all other things remaining the same, when migrants come from households with low income, the probability is that remittances would have a more direct impact on poverty alleviation. The fact that poor people are generally also low-skilled no doubt constrain their opportunities to move. Also important is the extent to which the multiplier effects of remittances reach poor households in a country.

Remittances also help alleviate the hardships of poverty in another important way, although this has not received sufficient attention so far in the specific context of poverty alleviation. As mentioned earlier in this chapter, migrants from different developing regions, notably Africa and Latin America, have been traditionally sending collective remittances through their hometown associations or similar migrants' organizations to help build or improve community assets such as freshwater wells, schools and hospitals, and small infrastructure projects such as roads and bridges. To the extent that the poor have access to such basic services and facilities that might have been unavailable to them otherwise, this certainly reduces their hardships. There are also many cases where remittances may not be able to lift the poorest people out of poverty, but may nonetheless significantly reduce their hardships or the severity of their poverty.

Remittances are not without pitfalls: The downside

Despite its positive contributions to economic and social progress, including poverty alleviation, remittances are not without its pitfalls. Many of these pitfalls are already well documented and analysed (a few are also mentioned above), but some have been brought into sharper focus by the present economic crisis.

Some analysts have emphasized that the appreciation of the national currency due to inflows of remittances – a variant of the so-called Dutch disease – can dampen a country's exports, encourage ostentatious consumption and add pressure to its import bill. By making exports more expensive in foreign markets, remittances can also lead to shifts of resources from the tradable sector to the non-tradable sector; and if this slows down employment growth, as is likely, the pressure on emigration would increase. An estimate made in 2004 showed that in a panel of 13 Latin American and Caribbean countries, a doubling of remittances would lead to a real exchange rate appreciation of nearly 22 per cent (Amuedo-Dorantes and Pozo, 2004; Bourdet and Falck, 2003). Evidence from countries such as Albania, Cape Verde, Egypt, the Republic of Moldova, Portugal and Turkey lends some credence to concerns about the adverse effect of remittance-led currency appreciation on exports.

However, evidence also shows that in most cases, especially for large economies, the negative effects of currency appreciation on export growth and competitiveness were marginal. In the Philippines, it was found that exports rose rapidly in times of rapid appreciation in the exchange rate. One reason for this could well be that part of the remittances was spent on imports. Critical imports could be used to improve firm productivity and the competitiveness of tradable goods; access to remittances also makes it easier for the government to improve infrastructure for the export sector. Further, under a flexible exchange rate policy, any upward appreciation in the exchange rate should be manageable without much difficulty.

That said, for small economies with less-diversified production structures and a weak export sector, any remittance-led sharp fluctuations in the exchange rate could be a real problem. Many countries (see Figure 9) are in this situation. For them, the challenge is to take timely, proactive policies to overcome these constraints and strive for economic diversification (discussed below and in chapter 4).

Figure 9: Top recipients of remittances: in USD and as a share of GDP (developing countries)

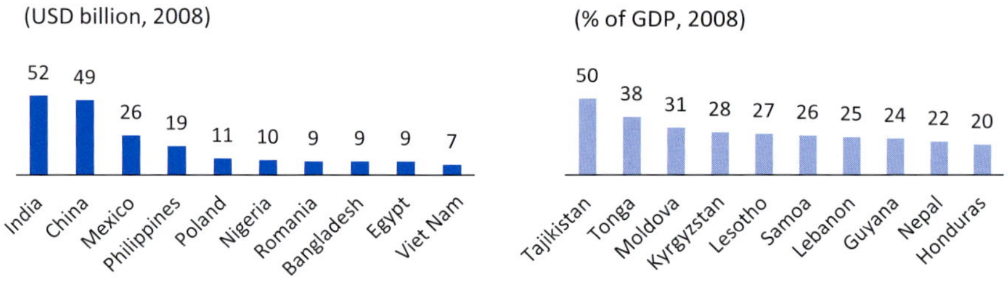

Source: Ratha et al., 2009b.

Another real danger is that excessive reliance on remittances may tempt governments to postpone essential but politically painful structural reform. As already noted, this may have happened in some of the remittance-receiving eastern Mediterranean countries in the 1960s and 1970s. This "brings distortions in the economy through inefficient allocation of resources, depress production of tradable goods and export-driven growth, and lead to further dependence on remittances, creating a vicious cycle and storing up trouble when remittances decline" (Ghosh, 2006). Trouble has emerged with the onset of the crisis, threatening to take a heavier toll on countries that have paid less attention to growth-oriented structural reform and diversification of sources of external funding and instead remained heavily dependent on remittances.

A decline in remittances adds to the difficulties of developing countries; for poorer countries that are heavily dependent on remittances, this could be disastrous

A sharp and continuing fall in remittance flows will adversely affect their positive role in the various areas mentioned above. While most remittance-receiving countries would suffer, the nature and extent of their difficulties would vary, with poor countries that are heavily dependent on remittances suffering the most. In 2008, India was the top remittance-receiving developing country, but remittances averaged no more than USD 30 per person and accounted for 3.1 per cent of the country's GDP. Although a recession-driven decline in remittances would create problems, especially for its current account balance (which is already in deficit due mainly to high oil import costs), India should have less difficulty in overriding them. This is because India has a high rate of growth, a relatively diversified and flexible economy, and several important sources of external revenue, in addition to remittances.[42]

By contrast, for a country like Tajikistan, where remittances provide a lifeline for the economy, a decline in remittances would be a cause for serious concern. The country's remittance receipt in 2008 was USD 1.6 billion, representing an average of USD 251 per person and accounting for 45.5 per cent of total GDP (World Bank, 2009a). A heavy reliance on remittances for its national income, a less-diversified production structure, and inadequate access to other sources of external revenue make Tajikistan extremely vulnerable. Furthermore, in the absence of adequate social safety nets, the poor are likely to be the hardest hit. The same concerns apply, albeit in varying degrees, to all countries where remittances constitute more than 20 per cent of GDP (see Figure 9). The fact that remittances are more stable than most other sources of external finance is hardly a consolation to these countries. As mentioned earlier, these countries would do well to diversify their production structures and sources of external finance, including, to the extent possible, tourism and trade, while making sure that remittances are effectively used (this is further discussed in the next chapter).

As the global economic crisis drives remittances down, making them pro-cyclical, countries heavily dependent on remittances will become highly vulnerable

The perils of heavy reliance on remittances are exacerbated when both host and home countries face serious economic woes and remittance behaviour becomes pro-cyclical. Many analysts tend to emphasize the counter-cyclicality of remittances. There is little doubt that during normal business cycles, remittances can well be counter-cyclical. When home countries face economic difficulties or natural disasters, many migrants would be inclined to send more to help those left behind. Evidence also shows that, with some

[42] This does not preclude the fact that the economic difficulties at the local level would be more serious for a few Indian states like Kerala that normally have high rates of emigration and remittances inflows.

exceptions, the downturn in the host country during a normal business cycle may not adversely affect the capacity or willingness of migrants to remit more to their homeland. However, this is subject to two important caveats. First, when business conditions are bad in the home country, it is most likely that remittances that are investment-oriented would decline due to risk-aversion on the part of most migrants. As already noted, even family-oriented remittances often include a component for small investments, be it on housing, farm improvement or microenterprise activities. Risk aversion may lead many migrants to withhold that part of the remittances until business conditions improve at home. Limits to counter-cyclicality also stem from the fact that when economic conditions in the homeland are bad, some of the less essential consumption items such as those related to social and religious festivities might well be cut back.

Second, and no less important, the counter-cyclicality of the remittance behaviour of migrants assumes that the downturn in the host country is just part of the normal business cycle. However, when the downturn takes the form of a serious economic crisis, and many migrants are fearful of losing their jobs or have already become jobless and their own future looks uncertain, they may be impelled to cut back on remittances. As noted, this was already happening with many Mexican migrants in the United States. Anecdotal evidence also suggests that some Mexican families at home were sending money to support members of their families who have migrated to the United States (McCabe and Meissner, 2010).

3.4 When both home and host countries face common problems and perils

Although separately presented under host and home countries, many of the negative effects of recession-induced changes in migration patterns could affect both groups of countries. It is not difficult to understand why or how in an increasingly globalizing world, improvement in one part of the economy would help the other parts, just as setbacks in one group of countries could rebound on another. In some cases, as illustrated below, the difficulties specific to each group could conflate and generate a third range of common problems.

Could rising social conflicts be a threat to global stability?

High unemployment and economic insecurity, especially among young workers, as discussed in chapters 1 and 2, already led to street protests in countries as varied as Greece, Iceland, and Latvia and contributed to labour strikes in France, the Russian Federation and the UK. Some of the, until recently, fast-growing countries were undergoing similar social turmoil.

China had witnessed dozens of protests at individual factories, though these were not as large as protests in Greece or the Baltic states, and Chinese government agencies expressed concern over the long march of 20 million migrant workers from rural areas. There were food riots in India, labour strikes in factories in Indonesia and protests in Chile.

Some have expressed concern that the situation could create global instability and threaten security. In February 2009, the new US director of national intelligence, Denis Blair, for example, told the US Congress that the instability caused by the global economic crisis had become the biggest security threat facing the United States, outpacing terrorism (*The New York Times*, 2009a). Mr Blair's statement may have been a little hyperbolic, but there are two interrelated aspects of security that cannot be lightly dismissed. This relates to the rise in irregular migration and human trafficking.

It has been noted that economic woes, lack of social safety nets and threats to livelihood may impel many desperate people in poor countries to seek escape outside their home country. Given the dwindling opportunities for legal entry in destination countries, especially for those who are poor and low-skilled, these desperate people would opt for irregular migration channels, fuelling human trafficking. The entry or attempted entry of large numbers of unwanted migrants, in defiance of the national laws of a destination country that is already under domestic social tension, could easily give rise to anti-immigrant feeling and encourage xenophobia. Should this happen, it could sow the seeds of misunderstanding between destination and origin countries and may lead to inter-state tension and even conflict that could easily spill over to many neighbouring countries in a region.

Also, as discussed in chapter 2, high youth unemployment among existing migrants, combined with a relative increase in new flows of migrants of non-working age and of those with a lower employment outcome, is another source of serious concern. As noted, this poses an immediate and difficult problem for destination countries in terms of migrant integration and the social and economic costs associated with the new entries. Badly handled, these problems could add to the danger of social or ethnic conflicts, which could also have repercussions in origin countries; and this again could suck in other countries which have political or ethnic links with them.

Why stringent and indiscriminate restrictions on migration can harm both groups of countries

Migration is a valuable channel for scientific and cultural exchange that helps promote development and enrich human civilization. A marginal decline in emigration or a slight rise in return may not stifle such an exchange, especially given the trends towards transnational networking with diasporas abroad. The risk, however, is that if panicky restrictions on migration continue to gather momentum and their reversal is delayed (which, once restrictions are in place, is quite likely to happen, as discussed in chapter 3), potential migrants' links with diaspora networks for interaction could gradually wane, and channels for labour market information severed or seriously weakened over time.

If this leads to a sharp and sustained decline in migration, it would restrain technological and economic progress and inhibit the enrichment and flourishing of human culture; this can be detrimental to the interests of all countries rich and poor. Rich countries' problems of ageing and labour supply, social security funding and demographic decline would become more pressing over the medium term. They would also be denied much of the benefits of the new energy and dynamism, drive and innovativeness that migrants normally bring with them – and this at a time when rich countries would need them most.

Developing countries would also be losers. They would have less possibility of drawing on technologies already existing in rich countries through scientific and knowledge-based exchange. The rate of their technological progress would consequently slow down. Many would face declines in remittances, which in turn would retard development and make poverty alleviation even more difficult than it already is. Further, developing countries would have less access to the safety valve that emigration provides against public discontent due to joblessness and against the possible breakdown of social safety arrangements.

It has been noted that, given the significant wage and productivity differentials between them, movement of labour from developing to advanced-economy countries can, under certain conditions, yield significant global welfare gains, benefiting both groups of countries and the migrants themselves. With declining migration, all these incremental welfare gains would be foregone. Worse still, this could lead the way to economic isolation and protectionism, creating a spiral towards a stagnating world fragmented by narrow domestic walls.

This chapter has highlighted a series of possible negative effects of recession-driven changes in migration and labour markets. However, just as the darkest clouds can have a silver lining, recession too has some relieving features. It offers new opportunities for bold action; and by creating a more conducive climate for people to accept change, it makes it less difficult to take such action. These issues are taken up in the next chapter that deals with policy response, as well as in the concluding chapter.

4. Meeting the challenge: The response

4.1 Principles, policies and action

A distinguishing and redeeming feature of the 2008–2009 recession was the impressive array of measures that governments around the world took to combat it and the speed at which they did so. Not surprisingly, the fall in global output was arrested after five quarters; by contrast, output decline continued for a further eight quarters in the economic crisis of 1929–1930. This chapter reviews some of the measures already taken by governments to deal with the impact of the recession on migration, and offers some suggestions to improve the situation as the economic downturn continues to place heavy strain on the world migration system. These are presented more in the form of lessons learned so that they could also be useful in the future if the world ever faces a similar economic upheaval as it did in 2008–2009.

Balance immediate pressures and long-term needs in shaping policies

Balancing immediate downward pressures on labour markets, on the one hand, and long-term economic interests and labour market needs, on the other, should be a guiding principle in shaping labour market and labour migration policies during a global crisis. Panicky or knee-jerk reaction, such as the indiscriminate sacking or deporting of migrant workers or a sudden ban on all new migration using blunt instruments, could be wasteful, and could further weaken business confidence and retard recovery. Once anti-immigrant measures and sentiment take hold, it may take long to reverse the process, as was experienced in the United States following the immigration restrictions it imposed in the late 1920s and 1930s.

Bearing the above in mind, it would be wise to pursue flexible immigration policies that: (a) seek to harmonize declining current labour needs and anticipated labour demand as economic recovery begins and (b) facilitate integration of new migrant workers into the labour market as it evolves in parallel to the pace of recovery.

As part of such policies it would be desirable to: issue multiple-entry visas to temporary migrant workers that would allow them to go home without prejudice to their re-employment in the host country; facilitate diasporas' links with their countries of origin, including though short-term visits; relax rules requiring uninterrupted stay in the host country to acquire permanent residence or citizenship; and extend, if necessary and only on a temporary basis, the requirement of prior job offers for admitting new migrants to categories of occupations which are currently exempt from such requirement.

Avoid trade protectionism, including trade-related movement of service-providing natural persons, and other populist inward-looking policies and propaganda

The discussion in the preceding chapters has shown that protectionist policies and mutual retaliation can seriously harm all trading partners and deepen the negative effects of the economic crisis. It has been noted that studies in the United States have shown that the loss of jobs related to overseas government procurement would far outweigh the number of jobs likely to be saved by banning such procurement of American goods under the "Buy American" or similar provision. Mention has also been made that trade protectionism can generate a chain of retaliatory action across economic sectors that would be economically harmful for all the parties involved and could have adverse repercussions even on inter-state relations.

To illustrate further the counterproductive effects of such measures, the US Chamber of Commerce considers that retaliation by Canadian municipalities could cost American water equipment companies alone an estimated USD 3 billion in lost business, with consequent repercussions on employment. The discussion in chapter 1 has also shown the need for countries to coordinate their fiscal, monetary and trade policies. If this is not done, as was the case in the 1930s, or if some countries coordinate their policies and others do not, the consequences for both employment and migration policies could be unfortunate.

All this strongly argue for avoiding trade and economic protectionism and other narrow, inward-looking or isolationist policies. It is important to alert the public about the pitfalls of such policies by taking timely and pre-emptive initiatives.

Initiate and revamp policies that promote job creation and use proactive labour market measures

Consumer confidence and spending are key to both business activity and bank lending and thus to sustainable national and global recovery. Consumer spending depends largely on jobs and earnings. Experience shows, however, that job recovery generally lags behind output recovery and all indications are that the situation would not be different this time, given that joblessness and wage stagnation have been hallmarks of the present crisis. Hence, there is a special need for policy and practical measures to promote job creation in both migrant-sending and migrant-receiving countries. An analysis of the merits and drawbacks of some of the measures already taken or were being considered in various countries could provide some useful leads for future action.

Short-term work schemes: In rich countries, especially in Europe, one main line of action has taken the form of supporting short-term work schemes. Although such schemes are not new, they were being used in countries like Germany on a scale never seen before, with 1.4 million workers taking part in state-backed short-term schemes. These are no doubt useful in avoiding immediate, large-scale redundancies. According to some analysts, Germany's heavier reliance on such schemes explained why, by mid-2009, when unemployment in the euro zone had risen to 9.5 per cent, in Germany the rate was lower at 7.6 per cent (*Forbes*, 2009).

These schemes do have certain merits. They help companies to protect their human capital and save on new hiring costs when recovery begins. In inflexible labour markets, they are also the only way to save on labour costs. Workers, too, have some security and they maintain ties with their companies; in most cases they also have some earnings, although not full pay. In Europe, schemes devised by individual companies to shave staff costs without actually laying off people varied widely. Spanish bank BVBA's plan to offer five years of leave on one third of pay and British Airways' month-long "work for free" scheme were among such examples.

However, the drawbacks of these schemes should not be discounted. One of the main criticisms of the schemes is that in times of fiscal strain, they could be quite expensive for governments in cases where these governments have to take on a large share of the financial burden. Even more important, if used to cover a long period (in Berlin, for example, eligibility had been extended to two years), they can inhibit companies from restructuring and workers from relocating. Companies would be handicapped to recruit new workers with skills that are more closely attuned to the needs of industrial recovery. As discussed in the previous chapters, in several sectors, including manufacturing, the recession-driven downturn has been so severe that full recovery will call for considerable restructuring, based on research and innovation. Existing workers may well be short of the skills and initiatives required for this purpose.

Another important drawback is that retaining workers on the payroll comes at the expense of labour productivity. In Germany, for example, hourly labour costs, according to the German statistical office, shot up by 4.1 per cent in 2009 compared to the previous year, and this contributed to industry's loss of competitiveness.

For employers and governments alike, a wise strategy would therefore be to consider these schemes as useful but time-bound, short-term measures and apply them in a calibrated manner so that, even when needed to speed up recovery, they do not stand in the way of recruitment of new workers.

Tax breaks to promote hiring: Another approach to promotion of employment concerns subsidy in the form of tax breaks. A merit of this approach, which received considerable attention in both the United States and the UK, is that it encourages the recruitment of new workers, including migrants. However, it carries a risk opposite to that associated with short-term work schemes: it could encourage firms to sack existing workers and replace them in order to take advantage of the tax break. To avoid this risk, a proposed variant of the tax-break approach is rewarding firms which increase the number of workers on their payroll. However, this, too, has a drawback: while struggling industries and firms would find it hard to take on many additional workers, those that are growing would largely benefit. A 1979 study of the tax credit scheme in 1977–1978 under the Carter administration in the United States showed that companies that knew about the scheme and used it hired 3 per cent more than those that did not (Perloff and Wachter, 1979). It made a significant difference, but this difference can also be attributed to faster-growing companies that were anxious to recruit and therefore sought out information on the scheme.

Finally, a strong argument can be made in favour of a special subsidy in the form of tax credits for low-paid workers, as this helps those who are forced to accept precarious and low-wage jobs as a result of the recession and encourages new hires. These tax credits, too, have their drawbacks, however. First, the benefit would go to those workers who, in any case, would have continued in their jobs. Second, while tax credits alleviate poverty among low-income groups, they do little to encourage firms to hire new skills needed for modernization and restructuring.

There are ways in which some of the risks associated with tax credits for jobs can be avoided or at least minimized. Some analysts in the United States, for example, have suggested setting as a baseline the level of a company's full-time employment at a certain date in the past, say 30 September 2009 (*Financial Times*, 2009w). To claim the tax credit, a business would have to show an increase in full-time employment from that base. This would avoid incidences of companies delaying the hiring of new workers or firing workers and rehiring them to claim the tax benefit. Employers who planned to hire workers may be inclined to do so to obtain the tax credit. Nonetheless, in times of rising joblessness, accelerated hiring is of significant value and should be welcomed.

Like the short-term work system, all tax credit schemes are expensive, especially in times of fiscal strain and rising public deficits. However, with careful design of a tax credit scheme, the net cost can be substantially reduced – for example, by requiring a company to hire half of its new workers from among those who currently draw unemployment benefits in order to obtain tax credit. An estimate in the United States showed that if 500,000 out of 1 million new workers hired under the tax credit system came from the ranks of workers enjoying employment benefits, this would, even under a set of conservative assumptions, lead to savings of at least USD 3 billion for unemployment benefit funds (*Financial Times*, 2009w).[43] (Some examples of tax break measures taken by governments to promote job creation are discussed in the next section on stimulus spending.)

Proactive labour market measures: These measures are by no means new, but since the onset of the recession, a number of governments in both migrant-sending and migrant-receiving countries have initiated some additional measures or strengthened existing ones in new ways. France, for example, has set up a new agency to reinforce employment market services and active labour market programmes. In several European countries, companies are devising schemes to shave staff costs without actually laying off people. Short-term work schemes mentioned above sometimes include targeted retraining. Studies in Europe suggest that as a proactive labour market measure, targeted training for specific groups of workers (and sectors) is more cost-effective than generalized training for workers. The UK was planning to spend GBP 100 million in retraining displaced workers, and Japan announced, as part of a comprehensive policy, a package for extensive training of the newly unemployed in areas severely affected by unemployment.

A number of origin countries have undertaken proactive labour market measures as part of their stimulus programmes and mostly in connection with the return and reintegration of their migrants, as noted separately in this chapter. To alleviate the hardship of its jobless, China has announced a series of initiatives, including vocational training, expansion of rural health care and crop subsidies, to ensure livelihood for those returning from cities to rural areas. In several origin countries, including Bangladesh, Indonesia, the Philippines, Sri Lanka and Uzbekistan, governments have been actively exploring alternative markets abroad in which to place their migrants. These initiatives are useful, especially in assessing labour needs and demand abroad. However, as already argued, given the global employment situation and the overall economic climate, immediate entry opportunities are likely to

[43] Some economists, Martin Feldstein, for example, thought more money should have been spent to add to aggregate demand.

be limited.[44] There is also a potential risk that in their anxiety to secure entry opportunities for immigration, governments would downplay the protection of the human and labour rights of their migrants. As further discussed later in this chapter, this risk must be avoided.

Redesign or supplement stimulus packages with measures focused on job creation

Most financial and fiscal stimulus packages introduced by governments include some proactive labour market measures, notably for job creation. However, in most cases, the design of these packages does not seem to be sufficiently job-oriented. Not surprisingly, they have failed to make a real dent in joblessness, causing continuing concern both in the United States and Europe.

The IMF recommended a global stimulus package equal to 2 per cent of the world GDP, although it later clarified that its recommendation did not necessarily apply to all. However, an early (and incomplete) assessment of 32 countries made by the ILO in April 2009 showed that their fiscal stimulus packages stood at 1.7 per cent of their GDP, and even less (1.4 %) as a share of world GDP.[45] Stimulus as a percentage of GDP for advanced economies was only 1.3 per cent – less than half the percentage for developing and emerging economies (see Table 4).

The US stimulus package, announced on 17 February 2009, amounted to 5 per cent of GDP over two to three years; as of February 2010, a significant part of the package had remained unspent. The scale of stimulus in a number of developing countries, especially in East Asia, surpassed that of the West. In November 2008, in addition to increased credit through state-controlled banks, China decided to spend USD 586 billion to stimulate the economy – a much higher proportion of national income than the US package. This money was more quickly spent. According to Fitch Ratings, fiscal stimulus packages as a share of GDP amounted to 13.5 per cent for China, 8 per cent for Singapore, 7.7 per cent for Thailand and 6.9 per cent for Viet Nam. Among rich countries, Japan was exceptional in starting with a huge stimulus package with a planned expenditure amounting to 14.6 per cent of its GDP, although its impact continued to be limited.

[44] Among the few examples of success is the agreement on the recruitment of Filipino caregivers signed between the Government of the Philippines and Japan's International Corporation of Welfare Services.

[45] This probably did not take into account the "automatic stabilizers" especially in Europe, which automatically increases public spending as unemployment rises; nor did the assessment include the stimulus packages subsequently announced or envisaged by various countries, both developed and developing.

Table 4: Stimulus spending as a percentage of GDP

	% of GDP	% of world GDP
Total	1.7	1.4
Advanced economies	1.3	-
Developing and emerging economies	2.7	-

Source: IILS estimates based on IMF and various sources (GDP figures).
Note: Based on 32 countries with available information.

The April 2009 ILO assessment of the stimulus packages of 32 countries showed that advanced economies had allocated one third of their total resources to tax cuts, the employment effects of which were difficult to assess, and less than 3 per cent of their resources to direct employment. The share of transfers to low-income households, too, was relatively modest at 10.8 per cent. In the United States, some economists, Martin Feldstein, for example, thought more money should have been spent to add to aggregate demand, but many others were in favour of increased emphasis on direct but sustainable job creation.

Developing and emerging economies were spending 0.2 per cent on direct employment measures and 6.8 per cent on social transfers to low-income households (see Figure 10). However, the share of infrastructure spending, which has a significant employment potential, was quite high at 46.5 per cent, compared to 37 per cent in advanced economies (IILS, 2009). According to Moody's, every dollar of additional infrastructure spending means USD 1.57 in economic activity, contributing to both employment and long-term growth.

Figure 10: Composition of stimulus packages as a percentage of the total for selected countries

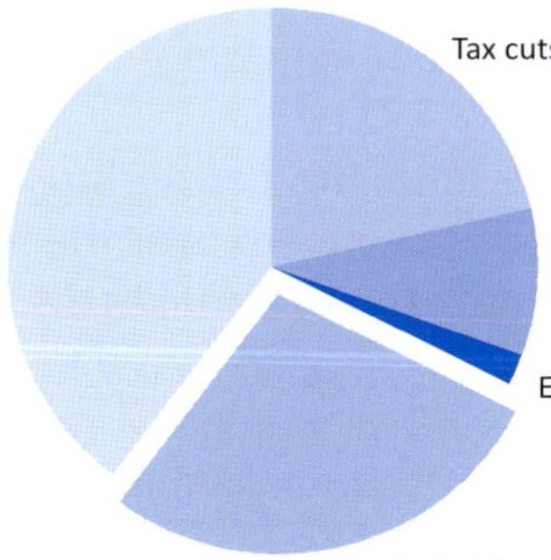

Source: IILS, based on Bloomberg, Asian Development Bank and *The New York Times*.
Notes:
[1] Based on 22 countries – 10 advanced and 12 developing and emerging economies.
[2] "Other spending" includes all other measures which are country-specific and/or difficult to categorize in the first four categories. Some of the components include, for example, direct/indirect help to businesses, indirect transfers for consumers, and increased funding for education and health.

As part of its stimulus spending to boost the economy, the Government of Singapore was hiring more teachers and health care workers and was also bringing forward construction projects that it had previously deferred.

Despite some modest signs of economic recovery since the third quarter of 2009, persistently high levels of joblessness have led, no doubt somewhat belatedly, some countries, especially the United States, to pay closer attention to job creation through special programmes involving both the public and private sectors. Following initial consideration of a USD 150 billion jobs promotion bill, the US Congress passed, with bipartisan support, a slimmer version of the bill, involving an outlay of USD 18 billion. It offers tax breaks to companies hiring unemployed workers – this is a step in the right direction, but it falls far short of what is needed. Analysts have estimated that the bill would generate only 250,000 jobs, making only a tiny dent in the 8.4 million employment deficit caused by the economic crisis. In the Republic of Korea, small- and medium-sized companies are the primary employers of migrant workers. In order to encourage these companies to hire more Korean workers, the government has announced a scheme to provide firms with a subsidy of 1.2 million Korean Won for every newly hired Korean national. However, this scheme excludes migrant workers.

In September 2009, the IMF estimated that the fiscal stimulus of 2 per cent of the GDP of G20 countries and temporary government spending will increase by between 1.2 and 4.7 percentage points in 2009. With growth prospects further improving, governments in many countries have rightly become more concerned about the extent of their fiscal deficit and the risk of asset price bubbles due to loose money. Fiscal deficits were projected to rise, on average, by 5.5 percent of national income across G20 countries, compared with 2007. Public debt was set to stabilize at 85 per cent of national income for G20 countries by 2014, but advanced economies would see their debt rise to 120 per cent of GDP, up from 80 per cent before the crisis.

As discussed in chapter 1, in the wake of the debt crisis in the euro zone, there has been increasing and legitimate concern over the huge fiscal deficit and public debt of advanced economies. This makes fiscal consolidation critically important. The credibility of the government's commitment to fiscal stabilization over a specified period of time helps rebuild business and consumer confidence. However, austerity alone cannot achieve this, nor can it be pushed too far. As part of a balanced strategy, governments also need to raise additional revenues to meet all their obligations and lend credibility to their own commitment to fiscal stabilization. This needs economic growth (see Annex II). It is also well recognized that increased growth critically depends on improvement in jobs and earnings and the increased consumer and business confidence that follows from it.

The incidence of public spending on growth remains a subject of much controversy among economists, however. The estimated growth effects vary from USD 2 of GDP per dollar (or even higher under certain conditions) to 70 cents per dollar of public expenditure. Much seems to depend on how, in which sector and under what conditions of monetary policy public funds are spent. Robert Hall, president of the American Economic Association, thought that in normal times the multiplier effect remains just under 1, but when monetary policy remains passive with a zero nominal interest rate, it could rise to 1.7 (Hall, 2009).

The US Congressional Budget Office estimated that USD 1 spent to help the unemployed created up to USD 1.90 in economic growth. To the extent that the calculation of the growth effect is valid, it makes sense to maintain support for job creation. The strategy for fiscal consolidation must therefore, for its own sake, include increased effort on the job front as well. An additional justification for this stems from the need for maintaining social stability at a time when people are under strain and intra-societal tension is high. It is now generally agreed that the extreme economic austerity that was imposed on Germany for paying reparation in the wake of the First World War made an important contribution to catapulting the Nazi party to power.

Consistent with a well-designed strategy to achieve fiscal consolidation, governments should therefore reallocate resources to programmes that have a direct impact on job creation, poverty alleviation and confidence-building. However, public spending on job creation should be highly selective. The emphasis should be on creating conditions conducive to job growth, but this should not exclude direct job creation, with attention being paid to ensure that such an effort does not crowd out the private sector. In some cases, such as large-scale infrastructure projects, it would be useful to explore possibilities of public–private sector collaboration. While creating jobs, many such programmes could, at the same time, promote long-term economic growth and contribute to energy efficiency.

Earmark some quickly deliverable funds to help tide remittance-dependent poor countries over a crisis

Most of the poor countries that were also heavily dependent on remittances found it difficult to develop robust stimulus packages of their own; and many in the same group of countries also lacked adequate social safety nets. As a consequence, the poorest in these poor countries have become even more vulnerable and their livelihoods seriously threatened. As argued in the previous chapters, if these countries lag behind and fall by the wayside while the rest of the world made progress towards recovery, this would mean not only large-scale human hardships but also social unrest and conflict, encouraging irregular emigration and human trafficking. Worse still, as failed or fragile states, these countries could easily fall prey to international terrorism.

These countries need some quickly deliverable aid that can be provided by making effective use of existing institutions. For example, a special account can be set up for this purpose at the World Bank, with the funds disbursed in cooperation with regional development banks. Many of these countries do not have enough budgetary resources, nor can they borrow easily in the international capital markets to launch robust stimulus programmes. The aid money under the special account could be used by these countries to promote targeted training and entrepreneurship development, direct job creation, infrastructure development and diversification of the economy, especially in countries that are now heavily dependent on migrants' remittances. Geared and targeted differently from the IMF's recently established "flexible credit line facility" to ease the external funding difficulty of emerging economies, the special account in some ways would complement the latter for poorer countries.

In the past, some aid funds have gone down the rathole, although in many other cases aid has played a valuable catalytic role in promoting development. For the reasons already discussed in chapter 1, prospects are far better now than in the past that the funds under the proposed special account would be effectively used. Even so, in order to ensure that delivery is fast and judiciously targeted and the money is well spent, it would be essential to: (a) establish within the existing institutional framework a special mechanism at the international and country levels; (b) formulate specific guidelines for planning and disbursement of aid; and (c) institute arrangements for systematic monitoring, evaluation and appropriate follow-up.

Crack down on human trafficking which could otherwise find an expanding market

At the time of writing, hard facts suggesting a serious increase in human trafficking as a consequence of the recession were lacking, although there was anecdotal and fragmentary information indicating that pressure for irregular information was building up. Also, both national and international legislation against migrant struggling and human trafficking is now well developed.

Even so, as discussed in chapter 3, there is a potential risk that, with the spread of economic woes to poor countries and shrinking opportunities for legal entry to destination countries, many people would be impelled to seek escape abroad through irregular channels. A good number of these potential migrants may then turn to human traffickers on their own initiative or they may be persuaded to do so by traffickers' false promises. As noted, lack of cash would not be a major problem; traffickers would welcome prospective migrants' personal bonds which would give them the means to ruthlessly exploit the victims and even their families for many years to come.

Given this possible scenario, governments should strictly enforce laws against migrant smuggling and human trafficking and, if necessary, tighten up existing national legislation. Precautionary vigilance should be an essential part of the process, in which human rights organizations, migrants' associations and other NGOs should also have an important role to play.

Strengthen vigilance against discrimination and the abuse of the human and labour rights of migrants and other vulnerable groups

Previous discussion, especially in chapter 3, has shown that a combination of factors, such as increased competition for jobs and resources; the expansion of the black economy, including sweatshops; and the presence of an increased number of irregular immigrants (holders of job-related visas who have lost their jobs as well as new irregular flows) could create a climate that aggravates the danger of discrimination and abuse of the human and labour rights of migrants and other vulnerable groups in host countries.

Special vigilance is therefore needed against the abuse of the human and labour rights of migrants and other vulnerable groups; this should include, in particular, precautionary measures against the arbitrary dismissal and expulsion of migrant workers. The fact that, as noted above, a number of sending counties have been actively engaged in promoting markets abroad for their migrants lends additional importance to this. Some analysts and human rights activists have expressed concern over what they consider a "paradigm shift" in the migration policies of sending countries from protective regulation to the promotion of markets abroad for their workers. It is encouraging that at least some of these countries, for instance, the Philippines and Sri Lanka, have tightened measures to protect their migrants' labour and human rights in parallel to their active search for alternative markets in which to place their migrants.

Governments of both host and home countries have a joint responsibility in the matter. If host countries have a responsibility to protect the basic human and labour rights of all those who are on their territories, home countries cannot remain indifferent to their obligations to their own citizens. The role that NGOs, including, in particular, trade unions, human rights organizations and migrants' associations, can play in this regard should not be minimized. Pertinent agreements signed between Sri Lankan trade unions and their counterparts in Bahrain, Jordan and Kuwait, with the support of the ILO, have shown an important new avenue for trade union action in this area (*Daily News*, 2009).

Take pre-emptive measures against the possible widespread resentment of foreigners and the rise of xenophobia

It is well known that in times of difficulty, when job losses increase and income falls, a host society's tolerance of foreigners tends to decline. The presence of a social underclass of foreigners, many of whom are in defiance of the country's established laws and regulations, could make the situation worse. These could be sources of widespread resentment against foreigners and give rise to xenophobia, which, in turn, could sow the seeds of social conflict and tension in inter-state relations. The situation could threaten national and international stability and retard global economic recovery.

An initiative to counteract the rise of xenophobic violence was the adoption of a law in August 2008 by Côte d'Ivoire to impose sanctions on conduct that incites such violence. In South Africa, a "no to xenophobia" mobile phone network was initiated in the wake of the May 2008 violence.[46]

Averting danger through vigilant and proactive measures should be the joint responsibility of both receiving and sending countries. As in other cases of possible human rights abuse, civil society, notably, human rights organizations, migrants' associations and trade unions, should be encouraged to play an active role.

Intensify efforts to promote the integration of migrants into the host society and, as far as possible, avoid cutting back on funds available for these activities

Financial constraints have led countries such as Ireland and Spain and several states in the United States to cut back on funds for integration activities. While the need for budgetary restraint in times of recession cannot be questioned, it would be unwise to consider migrant integration as a low-priority activity. As discussed earlier, in times of recession, there is an increased potential danger of tension growing between the host society and the migrant community. This can easily turn into social unrest and conflicts involving high economic and human costs. Viewed from this perspective, migrant integration acquires added importance in times of recession. Therefore,

[46] The impact of these initiatives is yet to be known. In the case of the law in Côte d'Ivoire, for example, the initial reception, according to some, has been lukewarm (see Zamble, 2008).

cutting back on integration funding should not be considered simply as an easy way to generate budgetary savings.

As part of migration management and integration, adopt special measures to facilitate the social and economic integration of young migrants of non-working age and those who, although of working age, have entered though non-labour migration channels and have low employment rates

The high level of youth unemployment among migrants (and non-migrants) has become a cause for serious concern. The problem is compounded in OECD countries which are set to witness a relative increase in the number of non-working-age migrants. If young migrants are properly trained and employed, they could be a bonus for ageing societies. To achieve this, it is critically important that they have adequate access to educational and job opportunities. If, however, they remain unemployed, disgruntled and victims of social exclusion, there is a real risk that they could turn into agents of disruption and conflict. Their social and economic integration should therefore be a priority concern of migration management. Special measures should also be taken to facilitate the integration of working-age migrants who enter through humanitarian channels, as they often face greater difficulty in actively participating in the labour market and getting jobs.

Ensure more effective use of remittances and encourage countries most heavily dependent on remittances to carry out necessary economic reforms to diversify their sources of external financial inflows

Efforts must be redoubled to encourage the use of formal channels by migrants to remit funds back home, to reduce transaction costs and to ensure more effective use of individual and collective remittances. Closer (financial and product) market integration linking remittance-receiving villages and local towns with other parts of the country should help transmit remittance-induced growth impulses to much larger parts of the national economy, enhance the multiplier effect of remittances and reduce the risk of local inflation. This should be an integral part of future economic reform in these countries.

It is important to sensitize countries whose economies are far too heavily dependent on remittances about the possible volatility and pro-cyclicality of remittances during global crises that seriously afflict migrant-receiving countries, even if remittances are more stable than some other sources of external finance such as private flows and development aid. These countries should be encouraged and assisted through such means as the special fund account mentioned above to carry out necessary (but generally painful and thus often neglected) economic reforms and institutional measures to diversify sources of external financial flows in the future.

Keep in readiness flexible arrangements to better manage the return of migrants, including returnees who wish to resettle at home, as well as those who seek to be redeployed abroad when recovery begins

Although so far there have been no massive return flows, as part of arrangements to deal with the volatility of migratory movements, including return flows, it is important that migrant-sending countries keep in readiness special schemes of assistance and training for: (a) those who wish to be reintegrated into the labour market and the wider society of the home country and (b) those who seek eventual redeployment abroad when the recovery begins and labour demand picks up. The proactive labour market policies mentioned above should be flexible enough to respond to the special needs of returnees.

As noted in chapter 3, past experiences have shown that the lack of such preparedness could throw the economy of the home country into disarray and lead to high human cost in case of the sudden and massive return of migrant workers. Turkey's 1973–1977 Five-Year Plan was in shambles when Western Europe put a sudden ban on labour recruitment in the mid-1970s. The unexpected repatriation of 1.5 million Egyptian workers and their dependents during the 1991 Gulf Crisis threw the country's budget out of gear, just as the sudden return of Indian migrants put the state of Kerala in south India under heavy strain (Ghosh, 2006). In the absence of anticipatory measures to reabsorb returning migrants, many would be jobless or withdraw from the labour market. Their prospects for self-employment would remain slim unless timely orientation and effective assistance are made available under a well-planned scheme.

The governments of a number of origin countries have initiated reintegration schemes or have expanded and reinforced existing ones. In 2007, under its National Plan for Human Development and Migration, the Government of Ecuador launched its "Welcome Home" programme providing an aid package to facilitate the return and reintegration of migrants abroad. Recent measures under the programme included an agreement with a university in Madrid to start a training programme for migrants returning to jobs in the agricultural sector, where there was a shortage of labour.

The Philippines has announced the establishment of an Expatriate Livelihood Support Fund to provide grants to train returning migrants in opening a small business; on completion of training, migrants can also obtain loans to start an enterprise. Likewise, Mexico (BECATE Programme of the National Employment

Service) provides laid-off migrants grants for training linked to small-business promotion. Both Kyrgyzstan and Tajikistan have launched programmes to promote domestic employment. Kyrgyzstan was planning new infrastructure activities such as hydroelectric projects to create jobs for returnees, while the emphasis in Tajikistan was on job creation through a multipronged approach covering promotion of small enterprises, rural employment and construction work. Arrangements were being made to provide training for returnees, develop entrepreneurship and grant loans to set up small enterprises. As regards rural employment, opportunities were being created for returnees to rent plots of arable land and training provided for jobs in rural areas. It was reported that by February 2009 a total of 150,000 jobs had been offered to returning migrants, including 20,000 in the construction sector (Radio Free Europe/Radio Liberty, 2009).

As can be seen from the above as well as from the sections on proactive labour market measures and stimulus spending in this chapter, many origin countries are setting store by the development of small enterprises for creating domestic jobs in response to falling emigration opportunities and also as a means of accommodating returnees. Small enterprises are generally labour-intensive and require relatively small initial capital outlay. As origin countries respond to the crisis, their focus on the development of this sector is therefore both understandable and largely logical.

This, however, also holds a potential danger that needs to be guarded against. Past experiences across countries and regions have shown that, even when initial capital funds are available, faulty project design, lack of careful market analysis, and inadequate technical, institutional and infrastructure support and systematic follow-up, often combined with the absence of prior business experience among returnees, can lead to the failure of many of these initiatives, creating an unfortunate backlash. Government agencies, the private sector and voluntary organizations can all play a part in addressing these deficiencies and constraints. The creation of one-stop shops as information centres, but not for specialized advice or services, is extremely useful, just as continuing monitoring of the progress and problems of ventures remains important to ensure their sustainable success.

5. Where do we go from here?

5.1 Can we turn the present crisis into a new global opportunity for the future?

The world migration system has been under increasing strain for more than four decades. The strain stems from the gathering mismatch between rising emigration pressures and dwindling opportunities for legal entry (especially of low-skilled workers). Instead of trying to bring these two powerful contradictory trends into a dynamic harmony through proactive inter-state cooperation, nations have followed mostly reactive and inward-looking policies and taken short-term or ad hoc measures to manage migration. This has produced a string of perverse results: the human and economic costs of mismanagement have risen sharply, while opportunities for enhancing world stability and welfare gains have been largely forgone.

The present economic crisis has worsened the situation. If joblessness and poverty continue to rise or remain at a high level in the coming years, derailing the MDG timetable, and if, instead of strengthening their cooperation, nations become more inward-looking and reactive in their migration policies, it would be difficult to avoid domestic and inter-state tension; world economic recovery, too, could be retarded.

Many of the policy and practical measures outlined in the preceding chapter would call for close and genuine cooperation between migrant-sending and migrant-receiving countries, both rich and poor, without which they will not make much headway. The pre-existence of an agreed international framework for the cooperative management of migration would have made it possible to avoid much of the extra strain that the crisis has placed on the migration system and the widespread concern caused by it. It would also have made it much easier to launch the necessary remedial measures through closer international cooperation.

As the discussion in the previous chapters has shown, there are now fledgling but ominous signs of anti-immigrant and restrictionist trends in both rich and poor countries. This might imply a further shift away from international cooperation. On the other hand, if the gravity and urgency of the migration situation lead nations to work more closely and initiate some joint action to meet the immediate challenge along suggested lines, this could very well open up a new opportunity for closer inter-state cooperation on a lasting basis and serve as a stepping stone towards the establishment of a common international framework for better governance of international migration.

Clearly, this would only happen if, unlike during the Great Depression, nations resist the temptation to become isolationist and inward-looking. The G20 summits in London and Pittsburgh recognized that global financial transactions, including banking, need better global governance. The agreement between nations during these summits to follow a harmonized global approach to the crisis and the acceptance of the need for international policy coordination to ensure orderliness, transparency and confidence in the financial sector, though still incipient, augur well for a similar approach for improving global governance of human mobility. In times of crises, just as nations could become panicky and short-sighted, they also become more willing to accept change. Sadly, though, unlike ongoing global efforts to better manage the financial system, no major new initiative has as yet emerged to develop a framework for inter-state cooperation to improve governance of human mobility (Ghosh, 2010).

The question could well be asked: How realistic is it to expect that nations would agree to adopt and adhere to a common international framework for managing migration? Three main reasons are generally cited as major constraints holding up the development of such a framework of inter-state cooperation: (a) the lack of a shared interest or a "common good" between origin and destination countries; (b) the absence of reciprocity of interests between the two groups of countries and asymmetry in their bargaining strengths; and c) the absence of a hegemonic power to sponsor and safeguard such a regime (Ghosh, 2007, 2009a).

How valid are these arguments?

Here are the replies:

All civilized states have a collective as well as an individual stake in maintaining international stability and peace and promoting economic progress. Orderliness and predictability of human mobility are among the essential conditions for achieving these goals, and these thus constitute the "common good" to underpin a global agreement on migration, fully in keeping with the tenets of regime theories.

This overall common stake does not preclude the fact that individual states also have differing, even conflicting, interests on many individual issues, depending on the country-specific situation and the type of migratory flows. However, it is precisely this diversity of state interests that offers, especially for labour migration, a huge potential for bargaining based on trade-off or reciprocity, as practiced in trade negotiations, making each country a potential net gainer at the end of the deal.

Among the areas of such reciprocity are: trade-offs between opportunities for legal entry in destination countries and the readmission of irregular migrants by countries of origin; between the availability of negotiated categories of skilled personnel from origin countries in exchange for destination countries' acceptance of some of the origin countries' less-skilled workers; and between the unmet labour demand in host countries' seasonal industries and occupations generally shunned by locals and the predictable supply of such labour from origin countries. Some scope also exists for negotiating reciprocity between the movement of high-level personnel from rich countries as intracompany transfers under Mode 3 (commercial presence) of the General Agreement on Trade in Services (GATS) and the temporary entry into industrial countries of service-providing professionals from developing countries both as employees (Mode 4) and as self-employed persons.

Additionally, significant trade-offs can be worked out between predictable labour supply from origin countries and alleviation, at least in the short to medium term (see below), of the growing strain on social security funding and the looming threat of demographic decline in receiving (industrial) countries. Reciprocity of interests across sectors (e.g. selective but additional access to the labour markets of destination countries in exchange for liberalization of specific product markets in origin countries) – a possibility recently discussed as part of the Doha Round of trade talks – also holds some significant promise. Interlocking reciprocal interests in these and other potential areas play a part in ensuring a high degree of symmetry in the bargaining powers of the two groups.

Since more and more countries – at least 25 per cent, according to a 1999 global survey by the ILO – are sending and receiving migrants at the same time, the protection and fair treatment of immigrants (and avoidance of tit-for-tat practices) also becomes an important area of reciprocal interests. Although often ignored or forgotten, it is useful to note that this is also an important element that makes the protection of migrants' human rights and good governance of human mobility closely interwoven.[47]

Although the principle of reciprocity of interests has underpinned some of the existing bilateral agreements between migrant-sending and migrant-receiving countries – as in the case, for example, of readmission agreements – its full potential for building inter-state cooperation still remains to be explored. Outside the EU, formal reciprocal commitments have generally been confined to such issues as readmission, remittances and targeted recruitment, and have taken place in a bilateral or subregional/regional setting. Unlike in the

[47] For a detailed discussion, see Ghosh (2003).

case of trade, neither governments nor intergovernmental organizations have explored the range of reciprocity that can be negotiated within the migration area and across sectors, providing an enduring basis for inter-state cooperation.

A basis for inter-state cooperation on labour migration

In a study on economic migration, Joel Trachtman of the Fletcher School of Law and Diplomacy (referred to above) draws up the structure of a multilateral legal framework for labour migration, within which states could negotiate commitments based on reciprocity of interests and unlock significant mutual and global welfare gains (Trachtman, 2009). In doing so, Professor Trachtman follows a positive list approach (under which each state specifies sectors or migration areas in which it would allow entry, taking into account its own conditions and interests) to commitments for openness. This thus ensures both the flexibility and gradualness of approach to openness and makes it politically more realistic.[48]

Both migrant-sending and migrant-receiving countries could benefit by giving systematic attention to this avenue of action and by developing their analytical research to identify various areas of reciprocity, as well as their negotiating skills to overcome bargaining problems and facilitate efficient cooperation, be it at the bilateral, plurilateral or multilateral level.[49]

As for the role of a hegemonic power posited in regime theories, the situation has significantly evolved over time, signalling a decline in the influence of one or more hegemonic powers in world politics, alongside the potential emergence of a multipolar world society. Not surprisingly, in recent years, several international agreements or regimes were initiated and/or subsequently sustained by collective initiatives in the United Nations (despite the absence of any exclusive hegemonic support or even resistance from one or more hegemonic powers). In such cases, collective consensus-building rather than hegemonic leadership had been the driving force. The increasing importance of the G20 in improving the governance of the financial sector is indicative of this trend.

If mutual confidence and commonality as well as reciprocity of interests are essential cornerstones of durable international cooperation in managing

---

[48] This is very much in line with the principle of "regulated openness" as envisioned under a predecessor global project, "A New International Regime for Orderly Movement of People (NIROMP)", supported by the United Nations and several European governments. See also Ghosh's foreword in Trachtman (2009).

[49] For a discussion of the reasons why a multilateral framework enjoys certain advantages over bilateral and plurilateral settings, see Trachtman (2009), chapter 9, and Ghosh, ed. (2000b), pp. 235–239.

migration, a multilateral framework, based on a set of negotiated and transparent norms and principles, is clearly the means to achieve this.

5.2 What will the overall framework of cooperation look like?

The overall framework of cooperation will be built on three main pillars: shared objectives, a set of agreed principles or norms and improved institutional arrangements at the global level for better coordination of migration management.[50]

The overall objectives of such cooperation would be to help ensure that the movement of people becomes more orderly, predictable and humane, and thus more manageable. Based on the principle of regulated openness and sustained by mutual cooperation between nations, the new arrangement will serve as a mechanism to help avoid knee-jerk reaction to a crisis-driven, temporary fall in labour demand or a sudden rise in emigration pressure. The new arrangement will seek to bring emigration pressures and the opportunities for legal entry into sustainable harmony. To this end, it will balance the needs and interests of sending, receiving and transit countries and the migrants themselves. The main tenets underpinning the whole approach include the following:

Labour-abundant origin countries shall take all necessary steps to reduce the pressure for disorderly and unwanted or irregular migration. Migrant-receiving countries, for their part, shall take appropriate measures to support the efforts of origin countries to reduce pressures for disorderly migration. In addition, they shall provide new opportunities for legal entry to meet their labour market and demographic needs, both current and projected. Both groups will meet their humanitarian and human rights obligations under major international instruments.

Both groups of countries shall adhere to a set of specific guidelines or norms to ensure coherence of policies and action to attain the above objectives. All countries will retain their basic right to determine the level of immigration in a flexible manner, but they will be guided by an agreed set of principles. To avoid policy contradictions at home or abroad, both groups shall ensure that the above migration policy objectives are factored into the formulation of policies in other related areas such as trade, aid, investment, human rights and the environment.

All participating countries shall take measures to make migration control more cost-effective and minimize negative externalities, including inter-state

[50] For a more detailed discussion, see Ghosh (2007), pp. 97–118.

tensions, associated with irregular and disruptive movements. They shall also enhance the credibility of the whole system of migration management by making national migration laws and practices more transparent and predictable.

The framework agreement shall be comprehensive to embrace all types of migratory flows, including labour migration, family reunification, asylum-seeking and other humanitarian flows, to avoid undue pressure on one channel and its clogging as a result of the diversion of migratory flows from some other channel or channels of entry. However, the agreement shall not supplant existing international instruments on various flows, but may reinforce or supplement any of their provisions, if necessary, to better achieve its overall objectives.

The adoption of the overall framework agreement should go hand-in-hand with better institutional arrangements, which are at present highly fragmented, at the global level[51] to ensure a more coordinated approach to migration management, including promotion of follow-up normative work and monitoring of the agreed instruments.

Forms of new inter-state cooperation

It has been noted that labour migration, however important, is one of the components of total migration and that the different types of migration are closely interrelated, so that the malfunctioning of any one channel could disrupt the effective working of one or more of the other channels. On the other hand, it is equally clear that each major type of migration has its own distinctive features and impacts and that they are not amenable to the same kind of normative treatment. Ideally, therefore, future inter-state cooperation should take the form of an overall framework agreement as a soft instrument (e.g. a solemn declaration). This should be supported and supplemented by a set of autonomous but interrelated sub-regimes in the form of soft and hard instruments, depending on the nature of the issues covered. Care must be taken so that these new sub-regimes, along with existing ones, are fully attuned to the broad objectives and principles of the overall framework agreement. The specific legal agreement on labour migration as discussed above should be an essential and integral part of the overall framework of inter-state cooperation.

[51] The scenario envisaged here is similar to the situation that combined the adoption of the 1951 United Nations Convention relating to the Status of Refugees with the establishment of the Office of the United Nations High Commissioner for Refugees. A roughly analogous example is the transformation of the General Agreement on Tariffs and Trade (GATT) into the World Trade Organization (WTO) alongside the signing of the Uruguay Round trade agreement.

Admittedly, as long as there are sharp economic and demographic imbalances between rich and poor countries, there is likely to be some tension in managing migration despite the existence of an agreed framework for cooperative action. The flexibility and gradualness embedded in the proposed approach would make it possible to tame much of any such tension and respond to any future shocks in the global economy, including those that may stem from climate change (this is further discussed in the concluding section).

Numbers versus rights: How valid is the premise?

The merits of the approach underlying the proposed overall agreement on cooperative management of human mobility can be seen in the context of some of the issues being raised in the contemporary debate on international migration. For instance, it has been argued by some that there is an essential incompatibility between "numbers" and "rights": the more the number of migrants through openness, the greater the risk of erosion of their rights and dilution of their entitlements. True, as discussed in this study, when origin-country governments aggressively try to promote markets abroad for their labour migrants, as some have been doing because of the recession-driven decline in labour demand, there is a real risk that they might be less exigent about the treatment of their migrants by host-country governments.

It should not be forgotten, however, that the same origin-country governments are claiming that they have also stepped up vigilance against infringement of the rights of their migrants abroad. This apart, the numbers-versus-rights dichotomy does not stand the test of the actual facts at least as a general premise. As a UNDP (2009) report noted, there is little cross-country evidence to support the hypothesis. Countries that have more migrants relative to the local population are often found to provide more rights and entitlements to migrants, and those which have seen an increase in their share of migrants over time have not necessarily cut back on migrants' rights and entitlements.

This is not surprising for several reasons:

First, the treatment extended by the host society and its government to immigrants is not just a matter of numbers of migrants. It is largely a reflection of its general attitude towards human rights and values as well; and the latter is shaped by a litany of factors, including the host society's own historical experience, tradition and culture, and internal social structure.

Second, the surrounding economic and political realities also matter. Consequently, attitudes towards migrants can change from time to time. As the long and chequered American history of immigration shows, in times of economic growth and prosperity as well as political stability and peace, a host society tends to be more generous towards immigrants, but less so in times of economic decline and political insecurity.

Third, and no less important, are the characteristics of immigrants. Levels of skills (and income), for example, can make a difference in terms of the acceptance and treatment of immigrants in the host society: as discussed in this study, skilled migrants generally are more easily accepted and they enjoy preferential treatment. What is even more crucial is the degree of the actual or perceived "otherness" of immigrants in terms of ethnicity, religion, language, social and cultural traits, and behaviour. When migrants sharply differ from the local population in these respects, the host society may fear losing its identity in the face of a large influx of migrants, and this fear can gain the upper hand over the "taste for diversity". In such situations, a host society may well be more stringent in according rights and entitlements to migrants, and the "numbers versus rights" hypothesis may then have a degree of validity.

The proposed overall agreement contains built-in safeguards against this potential risk in two ways. First, it specifically provides for state commitments on the protection of migrants' human and labour rights in keeping with major international instruments. Second, insofar as the agreement ensures orderliness and predictability of inflows and enables a destination country to avoid unwanted intakes, the "numbers versus rights" hypothesis ceases to be an issue. It provides a built-in and pre-emptive safeguard against the potential risk.

Is an exclusive demand-based approach to migration management adequate and sustainable?

The merits of the proposed overall agreement can also be appraised against the demand-side approach to migration management. A demand-based approach to openness in migration is sometimes advocated as a way of improving migration governance. During the EU's Swedish presidency in 2009, this approach was given a lot of prominence in the migration policy debate. In advocating for openness, especially for low-skilled migrants, a 2009 UNDP report (mentioned above) also suggested that this approach should be made "conditional on local demand."

It should not be forgotten, however, that a number of destination countries have already been following several variants, both and indirect, of this approach as part of their immigration policy. The tools deployed include: labour market tests, forecasts of future labour needs, use of shortage lists, application of a points system and the like. The importance of ensuring that the intake of migrants by a receiving country closely matches its labour needs is beyond doubt, but how adequate is the approach in and by itself to ensure the sound overall management of migration?

Experience has shown several limitations of the approach. One of the main difficulties in relying solely on it centres on the accuracy and reliability of the methodology used to assess and, especially, forecast the labour needs of a complex economy. There is general agreement that needs assessment must not be a bureaucratic exercise, nor must it be politicized. However, even with the active participation of independent expert groups and employers' organizations, assessments of future needs can go wrong because of high market volatility and rapid technical change. The boom and bust in an economy or a sector, as experienced, for example, in the IT sector in 2000–2001, can put even a carefully crafted assessment of future needs in disarray. The time gap between the assessment and the actual processing of applications for labour migrants can make the matter worse.

A rapid expansion of the informal sector in both rich and poor countries, accelerated by the economic crisis, presents another serious problem for an exclusive, demand-based approach to migration management. The informal economy, in which many small and marginal firms have subcontracting arrangements with well-reputed companies in the organized sector, accounts for a relatively large part of the total labour employed in a good number of countries. Many of them thrive (or try to survive) mostly by avoiding taxes and using cheap, docile and, to a large extent, irregular immigrant labour. Economic difficulties may make the situation worse as some employers who, in normal times, would not hire irregular migrants, may do so during an economic downturn in order to reduce labour costs (Bustamante, 1993). How does an exclusive demand-based approach handle this "distorted labour demand" (as I have called it elsewhere)? For obvious reasons, this part of labour demand is not likely to be included in a labour needs assessment exercise, and the serious and growing problem of the use of irregular immigrant labour in the informal sector will remain unabated.

This apart, what makes an exclusive, demand-based policy of migration management both inadequate and unsustainable is its narrow, unidimensional approach, as it deals only with cross-border labour migration and disregards all other migratory flows. However, earlier discussions in various parts of this study have shown how, given the close interconnection between different streams of migration, the fault lines in any of them can adversely affect the functioning of one or more of the other channels. To illustrate further, over the years, UNHCR has expressed its frustration over the difficulties of maintaining the integrity of the channel for asylum-seeking (refugee flows), as the channel was being clogged by those who were actually labour or economically motivated migrants. The converse is also true. The channel for entry of bona fide labour migrants could become clogged if there are fault lines in other channels of migration and these channels do not function well. This underlines the critical importance of a comprehensive policy embracing all of the different types of migration, not just labour migration.

Finally, even in dealing only with labour migration, the demand-based policy remains inadequate as it ignores the supply side and makes little attempt to bring the mismatch between the demand for migrant labour and the rising pressures for emigration into dynamic harmony. To achieve this, action needs to be taken at both ends of the flow by destination as well as origin countries within a coherent policy. An approach that is confined to the demand-side alone cannot do this.

The proposed overall framework of multilateral cooperation responds to both problems mentioned above. Unlike the unidimensional, demand-based approach, it is comprehensive enough to cover different types of migration within a coherent policy approach. It also recognizes the need for concerted action at both ends of the flows to redress the migration mismatch and lays down a set of principles as a basis for joint efforts by all principal actors to achieve this.

5.3 Migration in 2025: How will it look like?

It is conceivable that by 2025, the global migration system would become more stable and the framework of inter-state cooperation, if adopted, would work under much less tension, with the framework agreement itself contributing to it. The expected stability would come from three main sources. The *first* concerns declining pressures for emigration, especially through irregular channels, as a result of the high rates of economic growth and the improved political and economic situation, in general, in a number of migrant-sending developing countries such as China, India, Indonesia and Brazil.[52] This is likely to happen not just because of declining income and wage differentials between these countries and migrant-receiving rich countries. As I have argued elsewhere, more than the absolute level of income, it is the rate of economic growth and the pattern of its distribution, together with perceptions of the future performance of the economy, which influences the migration decision. As the economic outlook in these and several other middle- and low-income countries continue to improve, many people who would have otherwise moved abroad might prefer to stay home (Ghosh, 2005).

[52] Although a net emigration country, the Republic of Korea has already been through this transition, and it is now also regarded as an "advanced economy" under the IMF's income-based country groupings.

This, however, does not mean that intercountry wage differential is of no relevance to movements across borders. Rodrik (2002) estimated that average wages for similarly qualified workers in rich countries were 10 times higher or more than wages in poor countries. It can be expected, however, that in many cases, this huge wage differential would start coming down over time, as had happened in a significant, but somewhat different, manner between rich and poor countries in Europe in the nineteenth and early twentieth centuries. This time the process will be more complex, with internal development playing a pivotal role. This has already been happening in much of East Asia as country after county moved up the value chain and built up skills and capital. It is now happening quite fast in India at the upper ends of certain tradable sectors such as IT and pharmaceuticals. Between January and July 2010, each of India's top three groups in the IT sector had to increase pay by 10–20 per cent, and the cost relating to employees being poached by competitors hit a record USD 2 billion, according to analysts (*Financial Times*, 2010o). Recent outsourcing by a number of Indian companies to other developing and advanced-economy countries is indicative of this trend. In the export-oriented manufacturing industries, workers across Asia have become more vocal in their demands for better wages and working conditions.

All low- and middle-income countries will of course not economically advance at the same speed, but this would open up additional possibilities for intercountry movements of labour (and capital) within the developing world, and ease to some extent the existing immigration pressure on rich countries. The pattern of income distribution in most of these countries is no doubt highly skewed at present, but the increase in wages, combined with the expansion of public services, the development of infrastructure and the opening up of new economic opportunities, can be expected to improve the situation. Further, if these trends continue, they would attenuate some of the pressures for unwanted and disorderly migration abroad.

In some of the less-affluent countries, wages even at the lower-ends of the tradable sectors have been changing quite fast. Even in Bangladesh, a country known for its low-cost labour, workers in the clothing industry had demanded a threefold increase in monthly wages. In July 2010, the government finally decided to double the monthly legal minimum wages. The increase, effective from November 2010, would bring minimum wages in line with those in Cambodia, yet another low-wage country (*Financial Times*, 2010q). Even more significant are the recent developments in fast-growing China, which are worthwhile to note in some detail.

For years, China has been regarded as the workshop of the world, with its seemingly endless supply of cheap and pliable labour. However, pressures are building fast for upward movement of real wages. Although Chinese labour supply is still growing and the country has a vast reserve of low-skilled workers in its poor western regions, the number of young people (15–40 years old) entering the labour market is estimated to fall by 30 per cent over the next 10 years. Furthermore, the supply of workers under 40 years old has declined to as much as a fifth. This makes an important difference in labour supply and wages in China's coastal areas, because older workers are less willing to move from their homes in the hinterland. Cai Fang of the Chinese Academy of Social Sciences has estimated that while 24 per cent of rural workers aged 16–30 years migrate, only 11 per cent of those in their 40s tend to do so. In addition, some of the returnees are less willing to move out again. An official survey of returned migrants showed that 30 per cent of these people were not sure that they would repeat the venture, compared with 24 per cent two years ago (Cai and Du, 2009; *The Economist*, 2010b).

As factories move to the poor western regions of China to take advantage of lower wages and taxes,[53] local workers can find work closer to their homes, contributing further to labour shortages in Guandong and other coastal areas. Workers' move into the hinterland is also in line with the central government's strategy to spread the country's development into the vast interior. The process has started pushing up the prevailing low wages in these areas as well. Even younger workers are now less willing to move unless wages are sufficiently attractive. It will of course take time to make a significant impact on wages in the hinterland, given that some 40 per cent of the country's labour force is in agriculture, and productivity is much lower in this sector than in the rest of the economy.

Figure 11: China's tightening labour market

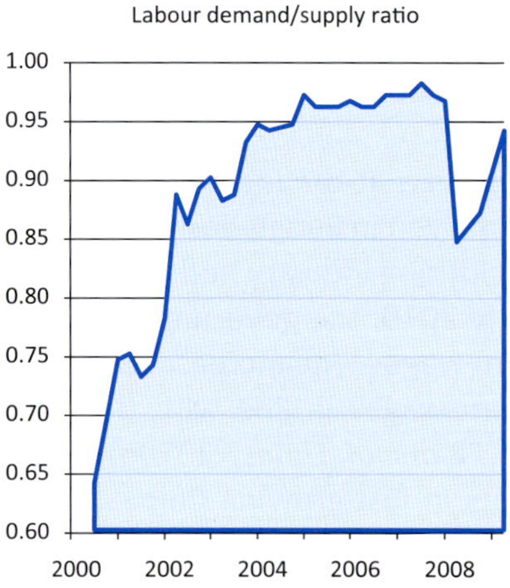

Sources: Financial Times, 2010ka.

[53] As this study was going to press, Foxconn announced its plan to move some of its production to a factory in inland Henan, China's most populous province, portending similar moves by other manufacturers.

Meanwhile, however, with the recovery of Chinese exports, labour scarcity is increasing in coastal areas, and workers are gaining bargaining power. Much-publicized strikes in Honda component factories in Guandong province and the turmoil following a spate of worker suicides at Foxconn, a contract manufacturer, have led to double-digit pay increases for workers at these companies, and fears have been growing over the spread of labour unrest. Unlike the first wave of migrants to coastal cities in the 1980s and 1990s, many of the current workers are not content with saving money for a few years before returning permanently to their homeland. Many would like to settle in cities, and they need higher wages to meet higher costs. As a consequence of these, the provincial government in Guandong has found it necessary to raise from May 2010 the provincial minimum wage by an average of more than 20 per cent.

Companies seem to be conscious of the fact that the recent wage concessions could signal the start of a period of consistent and large salary increases. Foxconn, for example, has announced a second, 66 per cent performance-related pay rise for its frontline workers across China from 1 October 2010, in addition to a 30 per cent increase announced earlier. As Terry Gou, head of Foxconn, put it: "Today we are going a bit quickly and moving ahead of everyone else, but when the adjustment to a higher wage environment comes, its speed and ferocity will be greater than you can imagine" (*Financial Times*, 2010l). The trend towards rising wages especially in coastal areas is likely to continue, especially since the government may also find it politically expedient to let this be so (see text box on the next page).

While the wage rise in coastal areas will attract workers from the interior of the country, it would also eventually (subject to liberalization of inward movement) attract workers from neighbouring countries with lower comparable wages, encouraging more South–South migration.[54] Trends of this kind would lead to an increase in the number and diversity of sending countries and contribute to the diffusion of tensions in the world migration system, at least those affecting the North–South divide. Further, over time, with the improvement of economic and social conditions in poor countries, the pressure for survival migration of low-skilled workers will decline, overall movements will gradually stabilize, and the stage will be set for the so-called migration transition to be effective.[55]

[54] It is also conceivable that, over time, some of the foreign and Taiwanese companies now operating in the China's coastal areas might move all or part of their operations to these countries.

[55] For a full discussion of how economic development interacts with migration, see Ghosh (1998), Appendix 1, pp. 177–181.

True, economic development in these countries will also encourage some new flows of migrants who might seek better opportunities in richer countries in the North (opportunity-seeking migration). However, these movements will be more a matter of choice, based on a rational assessment of costs and benefits than on economic compulsion. Opportunity-seeking migrants are likely to prepare for their move well in advance; they are likely to have adequate knowledge of the conditions in the destination country, and will normally avoid the costs and risks of entry through irregular channels. Fully in accord with the principles underlying the proposed inter-state arrangement for the cooperative management of migration, these movements will be more orderly, similar to those that now take place between rich countries in the North, with prospects of easier acceptance of migrants in the destination country. These new flows of migrants will run parallel to increased flows of trade and investment and closer interpenetration of markets. In other words, these movements will need to be seen as a structural feature of ongoing economic globalization.

Pressure for a rise in Chinese wages: Why the government should not be averse to it

Chinese workers in several plants in the coastal areas of China are trying to bypass state-controlled trade unions and staking their claims on higher wages through industrial action. Signs are emerging that the labour protests, which are already showing some success, could spread across the Pearl River Delta and the Yangtze River Delta regions. The Central government, however, has shown a high degree of tolerance and even sympathy for the workers' claim for higher wages. It is also worth recalling that, in 2008, the government enacted a labour contract law that required workers to be given written contracts. There are several reasons for this:

While the government, like the Communist Party, may remain anxious to avoid independent trade union activity as a parallel or an alternative pole of political power, it is conscious of the growing income inequality in the country and its potential destabilizing effect. The share of wages and salaries in China's GDP dropped from 57 per cent in 1983 to a mere 37 per cent in 2005 and has remained static since then (*Financial Times*, 2010kb). Both the government and the Communist Party have a stake in maintaining political and social stability, which can be threatened by a further increase in inequality.

The ruling Communist Party has maintained a ban on reporting the third in a series of strikes in various Honda factories, and the news blackout by local media seems to have continued. However, the underlying concern may well be to avoid a rapid spread of industrial unrest through coordinated action and the consequent social disruption if things go out of control. Significantly, an editorial in a tabloid with close ties to the Communist Party said:

> In the three decades of opening up, ordinary workers are among those who have received the smallest share of economic prosperity. The temporary stoppage of production lines in the four Honda factories... highlights the necessity of organized labour protection in Chinese factories (*Financial Times*, 2010j).

It is not very likely that the paper would have made such comments without at least the tacit acquiescence of the Central government. The attitude of the authorities to workers' claim for higher wages and improved working conditions is reflected in the sympathy offensive by Wen Jiabao, the Chinese premier. The official Xinhua News Agency quoted his statement addressed to a group of workers in Beijing as the strike continued at the Honda factory in June 2010:

> We must care for, love and respect migrant workers, especially the new generation of young migrant workers...Our society's wealth and tall buildings are embodiments of your toil and sweat. Your labour is glorious and deserves support from all society (*Financial Times*, 2010m).

If the Chinese authorities have a political stake in the workers' claim for higher wages, they could also find a reasonable wage increase economically acceptable, even useful. Many of the larger firms operating in China have ample room to absorb a relative increase in wages. Even for labour-intensive industries, labour costs are only a small part of the total cost. They possibly account for about 5 per cent of the retail price of China's main exports such as electronics and other consumer goods. According to Nomura estimates, between 1994 and 2008, while labour productivity rose annually by 21 per cent, wage growth was just over 13 per cent. Furthermore, profit margins for many of the contractors in China are higher than those for their customers in developed countries such as Japan and the United States. There is therefore little risk that they would leave China any time soon. Better wages would of course yield some benefits for employers as well as the economy, including, through higher retention rates, reduced recruitment and training costs, and increased efficiency.

No less important, China cannot indefinitely rely on export-based growth nor can it keep on increasing internal investment without an increase in domestic consumption. Rising wages are a sure means of achieving the latter. As rising wages also help the renminbi achieve real effective appreciation, they would at the same time help ease increase pressure from the United States and other industrial countries for an upward adjustment of the Chinese currency.

A second reason for the likely reduction in tension in the world migration system by 2025 concerns the rapid, largely unexpected and so far little noticed changes in fertility rates in both poor and rich countries. These changes portend that demographic imbalances may before long be a less powerful driving factor in intercountry migration. Excluding China, which has had a one-child policy since the early 1970s, in many parts of the developing world – such as Brazil, Indonesia, Iran and even in some areas of India – fertility rates are falling astonishingly fast (Bongaarts, 2009; *The Economist*, 2009b). They are racing through the demographic transition to reach the replacement rate of fertility that is consistent with a stable population. If, as seems likely, poor people would have greater access to population planning facilities, many more countries would join them. A number of countries in Asia and Latin America have a bulge of working-age adult population. Barring an untoward turn of events, this, alongside a falling fertility rate, would help these countries in both capital accumulation per head and rapid economic growth over the coming decades. At the same time, in an increasing number of rich countries, including France, Italy and Sweden, the fertility rate is rising again to reach the replacement rate.

The combination of these two trends, if they take hold and continue to remain valid, will have important implications for future migration. In developing countries, the decline in birth rates alongside economic growth will reduce demography-driven emigration pressure. At the same time, the rise in fertility rates in rich countries will lower demographic and labour market-related demand pull, which encourages immigration and, in the absence of opportunities for legal entry, opens the possibility for irregular inflows. Relative stability in population growth in both groups of countries should contribute to stability in migration flows.

Finally, stability in migration is also likely to be helped by technological progress and changes in the way of life in rich countries, especially for the younger generation. The increased use of labour-saving and automatic appliances for household work such as cleaning, housekeeping and gardening, as well as for low-skilled jobs in farming and industrial processes, should reduce the demand for low-skilled workers. These jobs are generally shunned by local workers in rich countries. The unmet labour demand pulls in low-skilled, low-wage immigrants from poor countries and, as this study has shown, often encourages inflows of irregular immigrants who are cheap and also more docile because of their precarious legal status. This, too, will decline in importance as a source of tension in South–North migration.

5.4 Standing at a crossroads

Could it be that the idea of better management of international migration through an agreed framework of inter-state cooperation is too optimistic? Is the scenario envisioned above too holistic? I would think it is not. The goal is certainly within our reach. However, much depends on whether nations – not just governments, but also the other principal actors, notably civil society and the private sector – are prepared to seriously take up the challenge of international migration, just as they have started doing to better manage global financial flows in the wake of the recession. Their response to pressing migration issues linked to the crisis may very well set the course: it could either open up new vistas of change for better governance of human mobility or reaffirm the old ways of trying to muddle through the migration morass. We are standing at a crossroads.

References

Adams, R. and J. Page
2005 Do international migration and remittances reduce poverty in developing countries? *World Development*, 33(10): 1645–1669.

Agrawal, A. et al.
2008 *Brain Drain or Brain Bank? The Impact of Skilled Emigration on Poor-Country Innovation*. NBER Working Paper 14592, December 2008, National Bureau of Economic Research, Cambridge, MA.

Amuedo-Dorantes, C. and S. Pozo
2004 Workers' remittances and the real exchange rate: The paradox of gifts. *World Development*, 32(8): 1407–1417.

Antal International
2009 *The Global Snapshot: A Survey of Hiring and Firing Trends in Key Employment Markets around the World 4*, September-October 2009, Antal International, London.

Bank of England
2010 *Quarterly Bulletin*, 50(1), March 2010. Bank of England Publishing, London, http://www.bankofengland.co.uk/publications/quarterlybulletin/qb1001.pdf

Barrett, A. and E. Kelly
2010 The impact of Ireland's recession on the labour market outcomes of its migrants, 2 June 2010, DELSA/ELSA/WP2 (2020)4. OECD, Paris.

Beine, M. et al.
2001 Brain drain and economic growth: theory and evidence. *Journal of Development Economics*, Vol. 64, pp. 275–289.

Bernanke, B.
1983 Non-monetary effects of the financial crisis in the propagation of the Great Depression. *American Economic Review*, 73(3), June 1983, pp. 257–276.

Blanchard, O. and C. Cottarelli
2010 The great false choice, stimulus or austerity. *Financial Times*, 12 August.

Bongaarts, J.
2009 Human population growth and the demographic transition. In: *The Impact of Population Growth in Tomorrows World* (R. Short and M. Potts, eds). Philosophical Transactions of the Royal Society B 364, October 2009, pp. 2985–2990.

Bonin, H. et al.
2000 Can immigration alleviate the demographic burden? *FinanzArchiv*, 57(1), September 2000, pp. 1–21.

Bourdet, Y. and H. Falck
2003 *Emigrants' Remittances and Dutch Disease in Cape Verde*. Department of Business Studies Working Paper 2003: 11, Kristianstad University College, Kristianstad.

Bustamante, J.A.
1993 Undocumented migration: a theoretical-methodological framework. Paper presented at the OECD Conference on Migration and International Co-operation: Challenges for OECD Countries, Madrid, March 1993.

Cai, F. and Y. Du (eds)
2009 *The China Population and Labor Yearbook, Volume 1: The Approaching Lewis Turning Point and its Policy Implications*. Brill, Leiden.

Central Statistics Office Ireland
2008 *Quarterly National Household Survey*, October 2008, Central Statistics Office, Cork.

Chishti, M. and C. Bergeron
2009 Recession breathes new life into US immigrant investor visa program. *Migration Information Source*, 15 December, Migration Policy Institute, Washington, D.C., http://www.migrationinformation.org/USFocus/display.cfm?ID=764
2010 Increasing evidence that recession has caused number of unauthorized immigrants in US to drop. *Migration Information Source*, 15 March 2010, Migration Policy Institute, Washington, D.C., http://www.migrationinformation.org/USFocus/display.cfm?ID=774

Daily News (Sri Lanka)
2009 Protection of migrant workers' rights: trade union agreements signed, 11 May, http://www.dailynews.lk/2009/05/11/bus20.asp

Davis, S. et al.
1996 *Job Creation and Destruction.* MIT Press, Cambridge, MA.

Dekle, R. et al.
2008 *Global Rebalancing with Gravity: Measuring the Burden of Adjustment*. NBER Working Paper 13846, March 2008, National Bureau of Economic Research, Cambridge, MA.

DeNavas-Walt, C. et al.
2009 *Income, Poverty, and Health Insurance Coverage in the United States: 2008*, Current Population Reports P60-236, September 2009, U.S. Census Bureau, Washington, D.C.

Desai, M. et al.
2001 *The Fiscal Impact of the Brain Drain: Indian Emigration to the US.* Weekly Political Economy Discussion Paper, Harvard University, Cambridge, MA.

Devan, J. and P.S. Tewari
2001 Brains abroad. *The McKinsey Quarterly No. 4, 2001 – Emerging Markets*. McKinsey & Company, New York.

Duran, J.
2008 *Economic Downturn Impacts Most on Migrant Workers*, October 2008, European Working Conditions Observatory, Dublin.

Dustmann, C.
1996 Return migration: the European experience. *Economic Policy*, 11(22), April 1996, pp. 215–250.

Eichengreen, B. and D.A. Irwin
2009a The protectionist temptation: lessons from the Great Depression for today. 17 March, http://voxeu.org/index.php?q=node/3280
2009b *The Slide to Protectionism in the Great Depression: Who Succumbed and Why?* NBER Working Paper 15142, July 2009, National Bureau of Economic Research, Cambridge, MA.

Eichengreen, B. and K.H. O'Rourke
2010 A tale of two depressions: what do the new data tell us? 8 March, http://www.voxeu.org/index.php?q=node/3421

European Bank for Reconstruction and Development (EBRD)
2009 *Transition Report 2009: Transition in Crisis*. EBRD, London.

Eurostat
2009 Euro area unemployment up to 9.7%. *Newsrelease-Euroindicators 153/2009.* Eurostat, Luxembourg.

Financial Times
2008a Skill shortages threat to oil supply, 30 July, http://www.ft.com/cms/s/0/a2edea88-5dce-11dd-8129-000077b07658.html
2008b Red Cross looks at cost-cutting round, 19 November, http://www.ft.com/cms/s/0/14e22ab6-b5d9-11dd-ab71-0000779fd18c.html
2009a World trade flows suffer as oil price plunges", 14 January, http://www.ft.com/cms/s/0/ee529ae2-e1da-11dd-afa0-0000779fd2ac.html
2009b Governments turn to barter deals as credit to secure food dries up, 27 January, http://www.ft.com/cms/s/0/989c6876-ec11-11dd-8838-0000779fd2ac.html
2009c Zoellick warns of fallout from bank guarantees, 28 January, http://www.ft.com/cms/s/0/336c973e-ecbe-11dd-a534-0000779fd2ac.html
2009d Downturn causes 20m job losses, 3 February, http://www.ft.com/cms/s/0/a6b47286-f194-11dd-8790-0000779fd2ac.html
2009e Rules of origin, 5 February, http://www.ft.com/cms/s/0/93619f42-f324-11dd-abe6-0000779fd2ac.html
2009f German engineering sector prepares for cuts, 11 February, http://www.ft.com/cms/s/0/0bbd9492-f775-11dd-81f7-000077b07658.html
2009g Violence adds to pain for jobless migrants, 13 February, http://www.ft.com/cms/s/0/3c275656-f971-11dd-90c1-000077b07658.html
2009h Nikkei Brazilians' struggle as social stock plummets, 16 February, http://www.ft.com/cms/s/0/d439a39a-fc4b-11dd-aed8-000077b07658.html
2009i Madrid police target illegal migrants, 17 February, http://www.ft.com/cms/s/0/403182fa-fc94-11dd-aed8-000077b07658.html
2009j US and Europe 'face prospect of new brain drain, 2 June, http://www.ft.com/cms/s/0/63c190a6-4f0b-11de-8c10-00144feabdc0.html
2009k Downturn slows tide of US-bound workers, 19 August, http://www.ft.com/cms/s/0/b34ade3c-8c57-11de-b14f-00144feabdc0.html
2009l Italy's foreign entrepreneurs show new face of immigration, 21 August, http://www.ft.com/cms/s/0/580e4574-8dea-11de-93df-00144feabdc0.html
2009m The risk of a double-dip depression is rising, 24 August, http://www.ft.com/cms/s/0/90227fdc-900d-11de-bc59-00144feabdc0.html
2009n Hoarders raided in India as prices soar, 28 August, http://www.ft.com/cms/s/0/5d565e06-936a-11de-b146-00144feabdc0.html
2009o Lamy says job losses will hit drive for freer trade, 2 September, http://www.ft.com/cms/s/0/b4194144-9758-11de-83c5-00144feabdc0.html
2009p View of the day: US jobless nears 10%, 8 September, http://www.ft.com/cms/s/0/10e5834a-9be3-11de-b214-00144feabdc0.html

2009q Leading economist fears double-dip recession, 15 September, http://www.ft.com/cms/s/0/dcb0d30c-a18e-11de-a88d-00144feabdc0.html

2009r Downturn puts paid to polish mobility, 16 September, http://www.ft.com/cms/s/0/99411a4e-a258-11de-9caa-00144feabdc0.html

2009s Europe turns to China and India for engineers, 16 September, http://www.ft.com/cms/s/0/bccf887c-a223-11de-9caa-00144feabdc0.html

2009t Poorest countries face 'long recovery', 17 September, http://www.ft.com/cms/s/0/59752584-a322-11de-ba74-00144feabdc0.html

2009u Trade becomes the poor relation, 24 September, http://www.ft.com/cms/s/0/5dcb0884-a7d6-11de-b0ee-00144feabdc0,s01=1.html

2009v Kroes warns EU over 'stealing' car jobs, 25 September, http://www.ft.com/cms/s/0/b66cbd3e-a93e-11de-9b7f-00144feabdc0.html

2009w Give credit to create jobs – but only where it's due, 4 November, http://www.ft.com/cms/s/0/fd432324-c8e2-11de-8f9d-00144feabdc0.html

2009x Fed dove warns of L-shaped US rebound, 11 November, http://www.ft.com/cms/s/0/541f8c3a-ce62-11de-a1ea-00144feabdc0.html

2009y Target to reduce hunger taken off summit pledge, 12 November, http://www.ft.com/cms/s/0/e6a74520-cf2a-11de-8a4b-00144feabdc0.html

2009z PM toughens stance on immigration, 13 November, http://www.ft.com/cms/s/0/ec79f99c-cff3-11de-a36d-00144feabdc0.html

2009aa Eurozone crawls out of recession, 14 November, http://www.ft.com/cms/s/0/c7a78376-d0bd-11de-af9c-00144feabdc0.html

2009ab Downturn deals blow to US immigrants, 18 November, http://www.ft.com/cms/s/0/d91e719a-d3e3-11de-8caf-00144feabdc0.html

2009ac OECD predicts a 'modest' recovery and rising job losses, 20 November, http://www.ft.com/cms/s/0/b70d262c-d574-11de-81ee-00144feabdc0.html

2009ad Chicago Fed chief sees 10.5% jobless peak, 23 November, http://www.ft.com/cms/s/0/41be5ad4-d7a0-11de-b578-00144feabdc0.html

2009ae Heed the danger of asset bubbles, 25 November, http://www.ft.com/cms/s/0/55fc4042-d962-11de-b2d5-00144feabdc0.html

2009af Europe warns China on trade backlash threat, 27 November, http://www.ft.com/cms/s/0/ff768ece-da62-11de-9c32-00144feabdc0.html

2009ag India's 7.9% growth spurt shatters forecasts, 1 December, http://www.ft.com/cms/s/0/bbdc8df2-dd74-11de-9f8b-00144feabdc0.html

2009ah Protectionism is gaining currency, 2 December, http://www.ft.com/cms/s/0/e8cdfefc-dee3-11de-adff-00144feab49a.html

2009ai China's urbanisation hits migrant workers, 24 December, http://www.ft.com/cms/s/0/91d82880-f02b-11de-833d-00144feab49a.html

2010a Wariness persists as Chinese exports rise, 12 January, http://www.ft.com/cms/s/0/92fdc522-ff1b-11de-a677-00144feab49a.html

2010b Concern as baby-boomers prepare for retirement, 1 March, http://www.ft.com/cms/s/0/a526d996-248c-11df-8be0-00144feab49a.html

2010c Brakes applied to protectionist surge, 9 March, http://www.ft.com/cms/s/0/180c65a4-2a12-11df-b940-00144feabdc0.html

2010d China exports rise seen as sign of robust recovery, 11 March, http://www.ft.com/cms/s/0/9cad211c-2cac-11df-8abb-00144feabdc0.html

2010e Data traffic outstrips mobile voice calls, 24 March, http://www.ft.com/cms/s/0/c6d6edce-3792-11df-88c6-00144feabdc0,s01=1.html

2010f Siemens seeks to stay ahead of Asian competition, 25 March, http://www.ft.com/cms/s/2/7136c562-37ae-11df-88c6-00144feabdc0.html

2010g Tough talk on China ignores economic reality, 1 April, http://www.ft.com/cms/s/0/dc113472-3cfd-11df-bbcf-00144feabdc0.html

2010h Skills shortage threatens German engineering, 20 April, http://www.ft.com/cms/s/0/3a782956-4c05-11df-a217-00144feab49a.html

2010i Temps leading the way out of EU recession, 2 June.

2010j Chinese labour is licensed to stake its claim, 3 June, http://www.ft.com/cms/s/0/9c959f2e-6ea6-11df-ad16-00144feabdc0.html

2010ka Chinese wages pose questions for exporters, 4 June.

2010kb Chinese workers are now in revolt, 4 June, http://www.ft.com/cms/s/0/a09746c6-6f3d-11df-9f43-00144feabdc0.html

2010l Foxconn to revise factory town model, 9 June, http://www.ft.com/cms/s/0/6d1f1614-735e-11df-ae73-00144feabdc0.html

2010m 'Grandpa Wen' seeks to calm restive workers, 16 June, http://www.ft.com/cms/s/0/1583df5e-78de-11df-a312-00144feabdc0.html

2010n IT outsourcing drives India's economic ascent, 28 July, http://www.ft.com/cms/s/0/227120e2-9994-11df-a852-00144feab49a.html

2010o New India's poster child grows up, 28 July.

2010p Vulnerable to vertigo-world economy, 28 July.

2010q Bangladesh lifts pay for garment workers, 30 July, http://www.ft.com/cms/s/0/93d65cee-9ac4-11df-87e6-00144feab49a.html

2010r Business attacks cap on skilled immigrants, 30 July, http://www.ft.com/cms/s/0/20bb8e8c-9b37-11df-baaf-00144feab49a.html

Fiscal Policy Institute (FPI)

2009 *Immigrants and the Economy: Contribution of Immigrant Workers to the Country's 25 Largest Metropolitan Areas, with a Focus on the Five Largest Metro Areas in the East*, December 2009, Fiscal Policy Institute, New York, http://www.fiscalpolicy.org/ImmigrantsIn25MetroAreas_20091130.pdf

2010 *Across the Spectrum: The Wide Range of Jobs Immigrants Do*, April 2010, Fiscal Policy Institute, New York, http://www.fiscalpolicy.org/FPI_ImmigrantsAndOccupationalDiversity.pdf

Forbes.com

2009 The big, German export gamble, 22 July, http://www.forbes.com/2009/07/22/germany-exports-manufacturing-markets-economy-unemployment.html

Ford, R.

2009 High-skilled foreign migrants entering Britain to halve, Jacqui Smith says. *The Times*, 23 February, http://www.timesonline.co.uk/tol/news/politics/article5784420.ece

Ghosh, B.

1996 Economic migration and the sending countries. In: *The Economics of Labour Migration* (J. van den Broeck, ed.). Edward Elgar, Cheltenham, pp. 77–113.

1997 Labour migration: causes, conditions, and consequences. Keynote paper presented at the World Congress on Globalization, Migration and the Labour Market, Nuremberg, May 1997.

1998 *Huddled Masses and Uncertain Shores: Insights into Irregular Migration*. Martinus Nijhoff Publishers, The Hague.

1999 Challenges and opportunities of economic globalization. Paper presented at the workshop of the Bundesanstalt für Arbeit, Frankfurt am Main.

2003 *Elusive Protection, Uncertain Lands: Migrants' Access to Human Rights*. IOM, Geneva.

2005 Economic effects of international migration: a synoptic overview. In: *World Migration Report 2005: Costs and Benefits of International Migration*. IOM, Geneva, pp. 163–183.

2006 *Migrants' Remittances and Development: Myths, Rhetoric and Realities*. IOM, Geneva and The Hague.

2007 Managing migration: towards the missing regime? In: *Migration Without Borders: Essays on the Free Movement of People* (A. Pécoud and P. de Guchteneire, eds). Published in association with UNESCO, Berghahn Books, Oxford, pp. 97–118.

2009a Inter-state co-operation and governance of human mobility: the promise and pitfalls. Paper presented at the Conference on Global Mobility Regimes, New York, April 2009.

2009b Foreword. In: *The International Law of Economic Migration: Toward the Fourth Freedom* (J.P. Trachtman). W.E. Upjohn Institute for Employment Research, Kalamazoo, MI, pp. xv–xxi.

2010 The global financial and economic crisis and migration governance. *Global Governance: A Review of Multilateralism and International Organizations*, 16(3), July 2010, pp. 317–321.

Ghosh, B. (ed.)

2000a *Return Migration: Journey of Hope or Despair?* IOM, United Nations, Geneva.

2000b *Managing Migration: Time for a New International Regime?* Oxford University Press, Oxford.

Goldfarb, R.S. et al.

1984 Can remittances compensate for manpower outflows: The case of Philippine physicians. *Journal of Development Economics*, May-June-August 1984.

Gott, C. and K. Johnston

2002 *The Migrant Population in the UK: Fiscal Effects*. RDS Occasional Paper 77, Home Office, London.

Hall, R.E.

2009 *How much does GDP rise if the government buys more output?* Brookings Papers on Economic Activity, Fall, 2009, pp. 183–231.

Hamilton, B. and J. Whaley

1984 Efficiency and distributional implications of global restrictions on labour mobility. *Journal of Development Economics*, Vol. 14, pp. 61–75.

Hanson, G.H. and A. Spilimbergo

1999 Illegal immigration, border enforcement, and relative wages: evidence from apprehensions at the U.S.–Mexico border. *American Economic Review*, 89(5): 1337–1357.

Hoefer, M. et al.

2010 Estimates of the unauthorized immigrant population residing in the United States: January 2009. Office of Immigration Statistics, Policy Directorate, US Department of Homeland Security.

Hoynes, H.

1999 *The Employment, Earnings, and Income of Less Skilled Workers Over the Business Cycle.* NBER Working Paper 7188, June 1999, National Bureau of Economic Research, Cambridge, MA.

International Institute for Labour Studies (IILS)

2009 *The Financial and Economic Crisis: A Decent Work Response*. ILO, Geneva, http://www.ilo.org/public/libdoc/ilo/2009/109B09_59_engl.pdf

2010 *Making Migration A Development Factor: The Case of North and West Africa*, ILO, Geneva http://www.ilo.org/public/english/bureau/inst/download/migration.pdf

International Labour Organization (ILO)

1999 *Migrant Workers*. International Labour Conference, 87th Session, 1999, ILO, Geneva.

2004 *Towards a Fair Deal for Migrant Workers in the Global Economy*, 2004, ILO, Geneva.

2009 *Global Employment Trends: January 2009*. ILO, Geneva.

International Monetary Fund (IMF)

2009 *World Economic Outlook 2009: Crisis and Recovery*. IMF, Washington, D.C.

Irish National Training & Employment Authority (FÁS)

2008 *FÁS Quarterly Labour Market Commentary*, Third Quarter 2008. FÁS, Dublin, http://www.fas.ie/NR/rdonlyres/9ABC5EE1-CF20-4AA5-ACA4-C5B81DD9FE5E/382/Quarterly2008Q996.pdf

Irons, J.S.

2009 How long would a job-market recovery take? Snapshot for January 2009, Economic Policy Institute, Washington, D.C., http://www.epi.org/economic_snapshots/entry/webfeatures_snapshots_20090107

Kennedy, D.

1999 *Freedom from Fear: The American People in Depression and War, 1929–1945*. Oxford University Press, New York.

Kerr, W.R. and W.F. Lincoln

2008 *The Supply Side of Innovation: H-1B Visa Reforms and US Ethnic Invention*. Harvard Business School Entrepreneurial Management Working Paper 09–005, December 2008. Harvard Business School, Cambridge, MA.

Kindleberger, C.P.

1973 *The World in Depression, 1929–1939*. Revised and enlarged 1986, University of California Press, Berkeley, CA.

Kochhar, R.

2008a *Unemployment Rose Sharply among Latino Immigrants in 2008*. Pew Hispanic Center, Washington D.C.

2008b *Latino Labor Report, 2008: Construction Reverses Job Growth for Latinos*, June 2008, Pew Hispanic Center, Washington, D.C., http://pewhispanic.org/files/reports/88.pdf

2008c *Sharp Decline in Income for Non-Citizen Immigrant Households, 2006–2007*, October 2008, Pew Hispanic Center, Washington, D.C., http://pewhispanic.org/files/reports/95.pdf

Lopez, M.H. et al.
2009 *Hispanics and the Economic Downturn: Housing Woes and Remittance Cuts*, January 2009, Pew Hispanic Center, Washington, D.C., http://pewhispanic.org/files/reports/100.pdf

Lowell, B.L. et al.
2004 *Brain Strain: Optimising Highly Skilled Migration from Developing Countries*. Asylum and Migration Working Paper 3, August 2004, Institute for Public Policy Research, London, http://www.ippr.org/publicationsandreports/publication.asp?id=295

Manpower, Inc.
2009 *Manpower Employment Outlook Survey Global Q4/09*, December 2009. Manpower, Milwaukee, WI.

Martin, P.
2009 *The Recession and Migration: Alternative Scenarios.* IMI Working Paper 13, International Migration Institute, University of Oxford, Oxford.

Mathematica Policy Research, Inc.
2010 *Hunger in America 2010*. National report prepared for Feeding America, January 2010, Feeding America, Chicago, IL.

McCabe, K. and D. Meissner
2010 Immigration and the United States: recession affects flows, prospects for reform. *Migration Information Source*, January 2010, Migration Policy Institute, Washington, D.C., http://www.migrationinformation.org/Profiles/display.cfm?ID=766

Menasce Horowitz, J.
2010 *Widespread Anti-Immigrant Sentiment in Italy*. Pew Global Attitudes Project, January 2010, Pew Research Center, Washington, D.C.

Mexican National Institute of Statistics and Geography (INEGI)
2009 La migración internacional Mexicana, más intense in las localidades rurales. *Comunicado 251/09*, 14 September 2009, http://www.inegi.gob.mx/inegi/contenidos/espanol/prensa/Boletines/Boletin/Comunicados/Especiales/2009/Septiembre/comunica.pdf

Migration News
1997 Congress: no major legislation expected in 1997. *Migration News*, 4(2), February 1997, http://migration.ucdavis.edu/mn/more.php?id=1151_0_2_0
2009a China: recession and migration. *Migration News*, 16(2), April 2009, http://migration.ucdavis.edu/mn/more.php?id=3510_0_3_0
2009b Southeast Asia. *Migration News*, 16(2), April 2009, http://migration.ucdavis.edu/mn/more.php?id=3512_0_3_0

Organisation for Economic Co-operation and Development (OECD)
2009 *International Migration Outlook*, SOPEMI 2009 Edition, OECD, Paris.
2010a The crisis and its impact on migrant employment and movements: drawing lessons for the recovery phase (DELSA/ELSA/WP2(2010)3).
2010b OECD Employment Outlook 2010: Moving beyond the job crisis. Paris.

Passel, J. and D. Cohn
2008 *Trends in Unauthorized Immigration: Undocumented Inflow* Now Trails Legal Inflow, October 2008, Pew Hispanic Center, Washington, D.C., http://pewhispanic.org/files/reports/94.pdf

Perloff, J.M. and M.L. Wachter
1979 The new jobs tax credit: an evaluation of the 1977–78 wage subsidy program. *American Economic Review*, 69(2), May 1979, pp. 173–179.

Pew Research Center
2009a *The Pulse of Europe 2009: 20 Years After the Fall of the Berlin Wall - End of Communism Cheered but Now with More Reservations.* Pew Global Attitudes Survey Report, November 2009, Pew Research Center, Washington, D.C., p. 59.
2009b *Troubled by Crime, the Economy, Drugs and Corruption: Most Mexicans See Better Life in U.S. – One-in-Three Would Migrate*. Report of the Pew Global Attitudes Project, 23 September 2009, Pew Research Center, Washington, D.C., http://pewglobal.org/files/pdf/266.pdf

Puri, S. and T. Ritzema
1999 *Migrant Worker Remittances, Micro-Finance and the Informal Economy: Prospects and Issues*. Social Finance Unit Working Paper 21, ILO, Geneva.

Radio Free Europe/Radio Liberty
2009 As work dries up, Central Asian migrants return home, 10 February, http://www.rferl.org/content/As_Work_Dries_Up_Central_Asian_Migrant_Workers_Return_Home/1490902.html

Rajan, R.G.
2010 *Fault Lines: How Hidden Fractures Still Threaten the World Economy*. Princeton University Press, Princeton, NJ.

Ratha, D. et al.
2009a *Migration and Development Brief 10*, July 2009. Migration and Remittances Team, Development Prospects Group, World Bank, Washington, D.C.
2009b *Migration and Development Brief 11*, November 2009. Migration and Remittances Team, Development Prospects Group, World Bank, Washington, D.C., http://siteresources.worldbank.org/INTPROSPECTS/Resources/334934-1110315015165/MigrationAndDevelopmentBrief11.pdf
2010 *Migration and Development Brief 12*, April 2010. Migration and Remittances Team, Development Prospects Group, World Bank, Washington, D.C.

Reinhart, C.M. and K.S. Rogoff
2008 *This Time is Different: A Panoramic View of Eight Centuries of Financial Crises*. NBER Working Paper 13882, March 2008, National Bureau of Economic Research, Cambridge, MA.

Rodriguez, E.R.
1996 International migrants' remittances in the Philippines. *Canadian Journal of Economics/Revue canadienne d'economique* 29, Special Issue, Part 2, April 1996, pp. S427–S432.

Rodrik, D.
2002 *Feasible Globalizations*. Working Paper RWP 02–029, J.F. Kennedy School of Government, Harvard University, Boston, MA.

Romer, C.
2009 *Lessons from the Great Depression for economic recovery in 2009.* Discussion paper presented at the Brookings Institute, Washington, D.C., 9 March.

Roosevelt, F.D.
1938 *The Public Papers and Addresses of Franklin D. Roosevelt, Volume Two, The Year of Crisis, 1933*. Random House, New York.

Roubini, N.
2009 The risk of a double-dip depression is rising. *Financial Times*, 24 August, London.

Shierholz, N.
2010 Labor market closes 2009 with no sign of robust jobs recovery. Economic Policy Institute, Washington, D.C., 8 January.

Skidelsky, R.
2009 *Keynes: The Return of the Master*. Public Affairs, New York.

Spatafora, N.
2005 Worker Remittances and Economic Development. *World Economic Outlook*. International Monetary Fund, Washington, D.C., pp. 69–84.

Strauss-Kahn, D.
2009 Successful partnerships for Africa's growth challenge. Speech delivered at the conference "Changes – Successful Partnerships for Africa's Growth Challenge", Dar-es-Salaam, 10 March 2009, http://www.changes-challenges.org/story/dominique-strauss-kahn-successful-partnerships-africa%E2%80%99s-growth-challenge

Sum, A. and I. Khatiwada
2010 *Labor Underutilization Problems of U.S. Workers across Household Income Groups at the End of the Great Recession: A Truly Great Depression among the Nation's Low Income Workers amidst Full Employment among the Most Affluent*. Study prepared for the C.S. Mott Foundation, February 2010, Center for Labor Market Studies, Northeastern University, Boston, MA.

Telegraph (UK)
2008 Small business face labour shortage as migrants quit UK, 2 November,http://www.telegraph.co.uk/finance/economics/3367907/Small-business-face-labour-shortage-as-migrants-quit-UK.html

The Economist
2009a Give me your scientists ..., 5 March.
2009b Go forth and multiply a lot less, 29 October.
2009c The great stabilization, 19 December 2009.
2010a Time to rebalance: a special report on America's economy, 3 April.
2010b Socialist workers: is China's labour market at a turning point?, 12 June.

The New York Times
2009a Job losses pose a threat to stability worldwide, 15 February, http://www.nytimes.com/2009/02/15/business/15global.html
2009b China fears tremors as jobs vanish from coast, 23 February, http://www.nytimes.com/2009/02/23/world/asia/23migrants.html
2009c Mexican data show migration to U.S. in decline, 15 May, http://www.nytimes.com/2009/05/15/us/15immig.html
2009d The peril of 'Buy American', 3 June, http://www.nytimes.com/2009/06/03/opinion/03weds1.html

2009e In unemployment report, signs of a jobless recovery, 5 September, http://www.nytimes.com/2009/09/05/business/economy/05jobs.html

2009f Recession drives women back to the work force, 19 September, http://www.nytimes.com/2009/09/19/business/19women.html

2009g Migrants going north now risk kidnappings, 17 October, http://www.nytimes.com/2009/10/18/world/americas/18tecate.html

2009h Everyman's financial meltdown, 23 October, http://www.nytimes.com/2009/10/23/opinion/23chernow.html?_r=1&scp=1&sq=&st=nyt

2009i U.S. unemployment rate hits 10.2%, highest in 26 years, 7 November, http://www.nytimes.com/2009/11/07/business/economy/07jobs.html?_r=1&scp=1&sq=trumka&st=nyt

2009j Across U.S., food stamps use soars and stigma fades, 29 November.

2010a The safety net: living on nothing but food stamps, 3 January, http://www.nytimes.com/2010/01/03/us/03foodstamps.html

2010b That 1937 feeling, 4 January, http://www.nytimes.com/2010/01/04/opinion/04krugman.html

2010c Two charged in deaths of immigrants at sea, 30 January, http://www.nytimes.com/2010/01/30/us/30smuggle.html

2010d Jobless rate falls to 9.7%, giving hope worst is over, 6 February, http://www.nytimes.com/2010/02/06/business/economy/06jobs.html?pagewanted=2&sq&st=nyt&scp=1

2010e America's real dream team, 21 March, http://www.nytimes.com/2010/03/21/opinion/21friedman.html?scp=3&sq=friedman&st=nyt

2010f Work force fueled by highly skilled immigrants, 15 April, http://www.nytimes.com/2010/04/16/us/16skilled.html

The Wall Street Journal

2008 Gates Foundation feels pinch from market turmoil, 25 November, http://online.wsj.com/article/SB122758023670855613.html

Trachtman, J.P.

2009 Negotiating global disciplines on migration. In: *The International Law of Economic Migration: Toward the Fourth Freedom*. W.E. Upjohn Institute for Employment Research, Kalamazoo, MI, pp. 271–296.

UK Border Agency

2009 *Immigration and Asylum Statistics Release*, 24 February. UK Border Agency, London.

UK Department for Communities and Local Government

2009 *Projections of Migration Inflows under Alternative Scenarios for the UK and World Economies*. Economics Paper 3, Department for Communities and Local Government, London, http://www.communities.gov.uk/documents/communities/pdf/1204238.pdf

United Nations Conference on Trade and Development (UNCTAD)
2009 *World Investment Report 2009: Transnational Corporations, Agricultural Production and Development*. United Nations, New York and Geneva.

United Nations Development Programme (UNDP)
2009 *Human Development Report 2009: Overcoming Barriers – Human Mobility and Development*. Palgrave Macmillan, Basingstoke.

US Department of Labor
2009 *Monthly Employment Situation Report*, September 2009. US Department of Labor, Washington, D.C.

VoxEU
2010 Diminished expectations, double dips, and external shocks, 13 September.

Williamson, J.G.
2002 *Winners and Losers over Two Centuries of Globalization.* NBER Working Paper 9161, September 2002, National Bureau of Economic Research, Cambridge, MA.

World Bank
1995 *World Development Report 1995: Workers in an Integrating World*. Oxford University Press, New York.
2005 *World Economic Outlook 2005: Globalization and External Imbalances*. World Bank, Washington, D.C.
2009a *Migration and Remittances Factbook 2008*, March 2009 Update. World Bank, Washington, D.C.
2009b *Protecting progress: the challenge facing low-income countries in the global recession*. Background paper presented at the G20 Leaders' Meeting, Pittsburgh, 24–25 September.

Xinhua News
2009 20 million jobless migrant workers return home, 2 February, http://news.xinhuanet.com/english/2009-02/02/content_10750749.htm

Zamble, F.
2008 Politics-Cote d'Ivoire: anti-xenophobia law gets lukewarm reception. *Interpress News Service Agency*, 21 May 2008, http://ipsnews.net/africa/nota.asp?idnews=43629

Annex I: The global economy and its outlook for 2010–2011: An update

As noted in chapter 1, the year 2010 started off with a relatively optimistic outlook for the world economy, marked by slow but steady recovery in most OECD countries and continuing progress in emerging economies. In its generally upbeat April 2010 report, the IMF expected the global economy to grow by 4.2 per cent in 2010 and by 4.3 per cent in 2011. The projected growth rate for advanced economies was 2.3 per cent in 2010, while the rate expected for emerging and developing economies was 6.3 per cent (IMF, 2009).

However, by the second quarter after this study went to press, things changed. The fledgling hope for sustainable growth in the global economy was largely dashed by a rising debt crisis in Europe. It started in Greece, but soon threatened Ireland, Portugal, and Spain. By April, it became a full-blown financial and economic crisis affecting the euro zone as a whole, with fears of its ripple effect spreading far beyond. The initial delay in dealing with the Greek sovereign debt made the problem much worse.

As the gravity of the situation became clearer, EU leaders rushed into action. Jointly with the IMF, the EU floated a USD 140 billion bailout plan to spare Greece from default, and soon thereafter, they designed a USD 923 billion fund, the European Financial Stability Fund (EFSF), with the IMF promising USD 337 billion as its share, to back up countries unable to tackle their debt situation. At the same time, the ECB started buying troubled countries' government bonds to put a cap on interest rates, restraining a precipitous rise in the debt-servicing burden of these countries, as well as to keep their bond market functioning. These measures, together with declared plans by EU countries to reduce their budget deficits, seemed to restore calm at least temporarily in the financial markets of Europe.

However, if relative financial calm returned in Europe, signs from across the Atlantic were becoming gloomier as the US economy showed new weaknesses. After having grown since the middle of 2009, it looked as if the economy might even shrink as growth slowed again to an annualized rate of 1.6 per cent in the second quarter of 2010. The economic gloom spread further by disappointing non-farm payrolls, which fell by 131,000, and came close on the heels of new softness in manufacturing activity and declining business and consumer confidence. In July, for the first time since 2009, Ben Bernanke, chairman of the Federal Reserve, told US Congress that the economic outlook was "unusually uncertain" (*Financial Times*, 2010p).

"Fiscal policy and inventory restocking will likely be providing less impetus to the recovery than in recent quarters," he added.

There were also other sources of concern. The United States had come out of past recessions with 6–8 per cent growth rates. However, this time, both growth and job creation were too weak to bring down the level of joblessness. There may have been reasons for this. Recent research has shown that when a recession is caused by a financial or banking crisis, recovery takes much longer than in the wake of normal recessions associated with business cycles. There is also some evidence that debt management or deleveraging during such crises takes several years. A paper by Carmen and Vincent Reinhart that examined 15 crises since 1977 showed that, on average, deleveraging took seven years (VoxEU, 2010). If the United States followed the same experience, its GDP would grow by 2.4 per cent over the next four to seven years. At that rate of growth, job creation should match population growth, but would make little dent in the backlog of unemployment. These calculations may not be fully valid – in fact, many economists do not agree with them – but they do reveal the nature of some of the difficulties ahead.

By the third quarter of 2010, there was also new turbulence in Europe. Although the measures taken earlier by the EU staved off an explosion, the euro zone's underlying problems were causing fresh concerns. Investors in bond markets were again demanding much higher interest rates for holding the debt of troubled countries. Ireland was particularly hit again because of the likely cost of bank rescues. More basic concerns were about imbalances within the euro zone between surplus countries such as Germany and those in the periphery, especially the PIGS (Portugal, Ireland, Greece and Spain). To many, the situation made the future of the euro currency itself somewhat uncertain. True, despite the headwinds in the second quarter, growth in the euro area – at double the US rate – was impressive, but this was mostly because of Germany's rapid growth (projected to rise to 3.4% in 2010) since reunification and the strong performance of Austria and the Netherlands. Growth in peripheral countries was sluggish or, as in the case of Greece, negative.

Many analysts felt that unless the structural causes of this imbalance were addressed, the future of the euro zone would continue to remain uncertain. There were also concerns that since growth in better-off EU countries were export-based, with the US economy slowing down and emerging Asia losing steam as well, the situation in Europe, including the UK, could be worse before long.

This turbulence in the world economy had already led some economists to believe that it was heading towards a double-dip recession. The uncertain outlook led to a heated policy debate on whether countries should increase stimulus to promote growth or opt for fiscal restraint to avert another debt crisis. The debate, however, was a false one since growth and fiscal stability were closely interlinked and the real issue was how to strike an optimal balance between the two (see Annex II), but it did create some considerable policy-level confusion.

Economists were also divided on whether or not the world economy was heading towards a double-dip recession. Already, in the wake of the gloom created by the European debt crisis, in the spring of 2010, even the IMF had recognized that there was a risk that if confidence and growth did implode in Europe, the negative spillovers to other countries and regions could be substantial. Using a test model based on previous experiences, the IMF estimated that world growth would then fall by 1.5 per cent in 2011 and the euro zone would suffer a serious double-dip. Since then, the weakness in the US economy, compounded by the gradual fading of the temporary boosts of inventory restocking and economic stimulus, and the cooling of manufacturing activities in emerging Asia, have heightened fears of a double-dip recession. Nouriel Roubini, for example, argued that a downturn in the global economy will accelerate in the second half of the year, and Europe and Japan will find it difficult to avoid a double-dip recession.

Many others, however, were taking a less gloomy view of the situation. They saw several positive trends in the global economy that they believed should put to rest fears of a double-dip recession. For instance, the EU was actively engaged in improving fiscal discipline and economic governance of the euro area, while troubled countries had embarked on credible fiscal consolidation plans. As for the United States, since recovery began, the economy had grown at a rate a little below 3 per cent. Although not robust enough to bring down the unemployment rate, it was faster than its long-term potential of 2. 5 per cent and was slowing at a more sustainable level. The slowdown of annualized growth in China (10.3% in the second quarter and 9.5% in the third quarter of 2010) and several other emerging countries were helping to maintain a balance between overheating and stalling growth. Furthermore, trade, which was likely to grow by 13 per cent in 2010, was showing new dynamism. These and other positive straws in the wind led optimists to shun concerns of a double-dip in the global economy. Experience also shows that once economies begin to grow after a downturn, they normally do not slide back into recession unless there are some new shocks.

What then is the conclusion? There is little doubt that, in 2010–2011, the global economy will continue to face several headwinds. Fiscal austerity could bite severely, stifling growth and raising social tension in Europe. Softness in jobs and housing was likely to continue both in Europe and the United

States. A major downturn in industrial countries could adversely affect the performance of emerging economies as well because of trade and financial linkages. At the same time, there was a growing fear in emerging economies that loose money in the form of low interest rates and quantitative easing, especially in the United States, would create asset bubbles and inflationary pressure that would be hard to control. Another serious concern was that imbalances in the global economy, especially between the United States and China in their current accounts and also within the euro zone, could encourage trade protectionism. The situation could worsen if the trend towards competitive devaluation gains further ground, threatening the cohesion of G20 countries.*

All this carries some real risks and will most probably lead to a slow pace of global growth and recovery. However, on balance, it is much less likely – and this is in line with the general consensus – that the global economy will plunge into a double-dip recession. In other words, in all probability, countries will muddle through the constraints; the speed of their recovery in 2010–2011 may well be slower but they may not succumb to another crisis. However, a disquieting and defining feature of the sluggish growth will be slow improvement in jobs and wages in the coming years. A projection made by the ILO in October 2010 suggested that advanced economies would need to wait until 2015 to regain the total level of employment that they enjoyed before the crisis. It concluded that this delay would increase social tension. Should this projection be correct, it will, in turn, have a significant effect on the pattern of international migration, with some disquieting social and economic implications for both developed and developing countries as outlined in the study.

* At its October 2010 meeting in the city of Gyeongju in the Republic of Korea, G20 finance ministers agreed to avoid competitive undervaluation of currencies in a push to diffuse tensions in trade and economic relations. The actual implementation of the decision remains to be seen.

Annex II: Stimulus versus austerity: A false dichotomy?

In 2009, at the height of the economic crisis, the leaders of the G20, meeting in London and Pittsburgh, pledged a fiscal stimulus plan worth a combined 2 per cent of world GDP to boost the global economy. Despite some initial hesitation of a few in Europe, G20 leaders lost little time in agreeing on the plan; this ushered in a new phase of policy coordination at the global level, in which, for the first time, emerging-country leaders took an active part. However, the situation soon changed. At their meeting in Toronto in June 2010, the same leaders pledged to at least halve their deficits by 2013. Though couched in flexible terms to allow themselves elbow room, the decision marked a significant change in policy stance – a shift from fiscal stimulus to fiscal consolidation.

There were two main reasons for this. First, the sovereign debt crisis in Greece and the fear of its contagion effect prompted most European countries to think that it was urgent to focus on fiscal consolidation to avoid a wider debt crisis. There was also a feeling in some circles that fiscal stimulus had played a part in boosting the economy and that further fiscal deficits would fail to boost demand. It would crowd out private spending and investment needed for recovery and could stoke inflation. Fiscal restraint would have the opposite effect of spurring business confidence and promoting investment and growth. It was therefore time for stimulus to exit.

Since then the debate on the need for further fiscal stimulus or quicker fiscal stabilization has intensified. Economists have expressed conflicting views; politicians in some countries such as the United States have tended to make the debate ideological; and the media have given the divergence wide publicity. However, the debate at its extreme is a false one. In reality, there is little conflict between maintaining support for growth and restoring fiscal stability. These two are closely correlated, and both need to be pursued in a timely and balanced manner. The real issue is that of designing and sequencing.

A country with an exceptionally heavy public debt cannot be expected to repay its debt within a reasonable period merely by cutting fiscal expenditure or raising taxes. It will not only be too onerous to do so; it can also make the situation worse by choking off growth at a time when growth is needed to increase revenue. It would be equally dangerous, however, if a country seeks to stimulate growth though additional public expenditure, unless it enjoys sufficient confidence in the capital market and can borrow at a reasonable rate of interest. This, in turn, would depend on its commitment to a well-defined and credible strategy to reduce fiscal debt over a specified period of time. In the absence of such strategies, the effectiveness of stimulus measures could be eroded.

The debate on the subject often gets confused because of certain misconceptions. For example, some of those opposed to maintaining stimulus seems to convey the impression that past stimulus expenditure had been a major factor in creating huge public debt for advanced-economy countries. This, however, is far from fact. True, by 2015, public debt for the G20 will rise at a rate higher than at any time since the Second World War. Advanced economies will carry a still heavier debt burden: their debt is likely to rise to 120 per cent of GDP by 2014 – up from 80 per cent before the crisis. Such huge public debt can make people nervous, but most of it comes from past fiscal deficits, compounded by the crisis itself. Only 10 percent of the new, post-crisis debt of G20 countries can be attributed to stimulus measures to boost their economies.

Confusion is also created when fiscal stabilization is equated only with simple budget cuts that inhibit growth. When planned fiscal stabilization includes structural reform, it can, in many cases, contribute to growth. For example, raising the retirement age, as some European governments have been trying to do, not just reduces governments' financial burden but also contributes to tax revenues and stimulates growth. In such cases, fiscal consolidation could also be growth-friendly. Likewise, stimulus does not mean indiscriminate fiscal expansion. It can also include, albeit increase total government expenditure, budget cuts on some of the low-priority and discretionary budgetary items, as the United States has planned on a small scale. It can also be better targeted to boost both growth and employment and encourage the private sector, which, as mentioned in the study, has not always been the case. In this way, stimulus can help fiscal consolidation by raising revenue over time. In short, there is scope for better designing both fiscal stimulus and retrenchment plans. When this is done, the contradiction between them would seem much less sharper than what some would like us to believe.

There is of course the real issue of timing. Some are strongly in favour of more fiscal consolidation now on grounds that market perception of government solvency can change quickly, which makes it necessary for countries to move pre-emptively. However, as Blanchard and Cottarelli (2010) noted, the argument cuts both ways. If hasty fiscal adjustment derails growth, government credibility could also be a casualty. The answer to this dilemma lies in pursuing measures for growth and fiscal consolidation in a balanced manner, avoiding the extremes. The exact sequencing and intensity of the measures would depend largely on the country-specific situation.

Greece, for example, had reached a debt situation where it had to rely more on fiscal tightening to regain credibility in the capital market. On the other hand, the United States holds the world's reserve currency, has huge private sector surpluses, and can still tap the capital market at low cost. It also has a large amount of unused installed capacity and high unemployment, lessening the risk of inflation. In addition, US recovery is still fragile and uncertain. The country, therefore, is in a different situation. At the same time, given that its public debt would jump from 63 per cent of GDP in 2005 to 92 per cent of GDP in 2010, the United States needs to have a convincing plan to reduce its debt to a sustainable level over the medium term.

In both cases, extremes should be avoided. Drastic and sudden cuts in budgets, without adequate safeguards to protect the poor, could ignite large-scale social upheaval, endangering both growth and governments' creditworthiness in the market. Likewise, if governments indulge in excessive increase in fiscal expenditure, they could quickly lose creditability and find themselves dumped by the market.

Policy coordination does not necessarily mean that all countries need to follow exactly identical policies. What it does involve, however, are countries adhering to policies that are, as far as possible, complementary – or, at least, as compatible and coherent with one another – in serving common objectives. Such flexibility should be an essential, built-in element of policy coordination simply because all countries are not exactly in the same situation.

Annex III: Outlook for remittance flows to developing countries, 2011

	2006	2007	2008	2009e	2010f	2011f
USD billion						
Developing countries	**235**	**290**	**336**	**316**	**335**	**359**
East Asia and Pacific	58	71	86	86	94	103
Europe and Central Asia	37	51	58	46	48	52
Latin America and Caribbean	59	63	64	57	60	64
Middle East and North Africa	26	32	35	32	33	34
South Asia	43	54	72	75	79	83
Sub-Saharan Africa	13	19	21	21	22	23
Low-income countries	20	25	32	32	35	37
Middle-income countries	215	265	304	283	301	322
World	317	385	443	414	437	465
Growth rate (%)						
Developing countries	**18.4%**	**23.1%**	**15.9%**	**-6.0%**	**6.2%**	**7.1%**
East Asia and Pacific	14.2%	23.8%	20.7%	-0.4%	9.8%	9.2%
Europe and Central Asia	24.1%	36.0%	13.3%	-20.7%	5.4%	7.6%
Latin America and Caribbean	18.1%	6.9%	2.1%	-12.3%	5.7%	7.9%
Middle East and North Africa	4.6%	21.4%	9.8%	-8.1%	3.6%	4.0%
South Asia	25.3%	27.1%	32.6%	4.9%	4.7%	5.2%
Sub-Saharan Africa	34.8%	48.5%	14.1%	-2.7%	4.4%	5.8%
Low-income countries	23.9%	24.0%	29.4%	1.0%	7.2%	7.7%
Middle-income countries	17.9%	23.0%	14.7%	-6.7%	6.1%	7.0%
World	15.6%	21.4%	15.0%	-6.7%	5.7%	6.3%

Source: Ratha et al., 2010
Note: e = estimate; f = forecast